HIP
HOTELS

USA

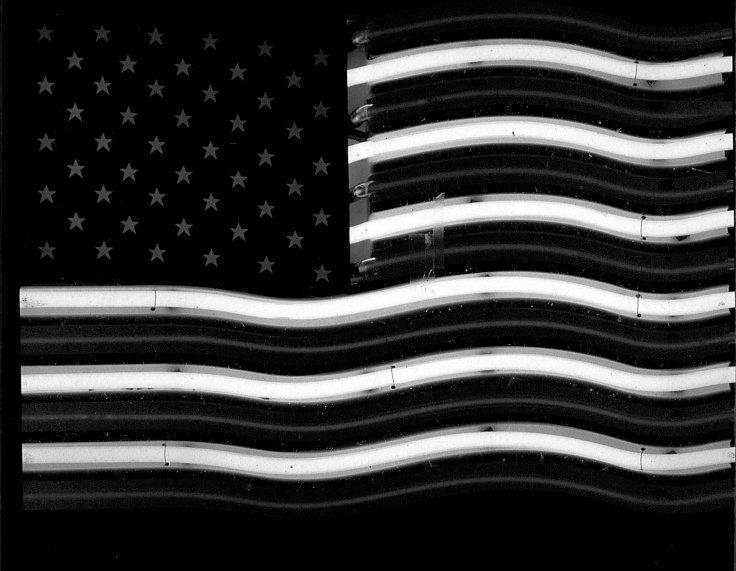

HERBERT YPMA

HIP
HOTELS

with 474 illustrations, 357 in color

Thames & Hudson

introduction

"America the Beautiful." Ever since I was in elementary school, in a tiny town an hour north of Manhattan, this song has for me summed up the United States.

It was an impression fueled by some serious mileage. By the time I was thirteen, I had been to every state in the Union except for Alaska and Hawaii. While my classmates were off at camp for the summer, I was in the back of the family Jeep, criss-crossing the country, north, south, east and west, en route to and from my geologist father's field trips. These excursions usually lasted all summer, and what remains their most vivid memory is the spectacle of America's natural beauty. The towering monumentality of California's redwood forests, the striped sandy cliffs of Snake River Canyon, the bubbling hot springs of the high Colorado Rockies, the geysers and bears of Yellowstone, the vast emptiness of Montana, the dark dense forests around the Great Lakes: all these sights are now as clichéd as the Eiffel Tower or Big Ben. But cliché or no, the sheer diversity and amplitude of America's natural beauty remains breathtaking.

It can come as a surprise to non-Americans that so few US citizens own a passport (under 20%); but then few non-Americans grasp what amazing experiences lie right on Americans' doorsteps. It is not just the landscape that varies so dramatically. The climate, the cuisine and the culture differ from state to state. New Yorkers are tough, Californians are mellow, Southerners remain more formal, while Texans are straight-talking, even brash. The locals of Montana are as surprised and curious to see a New York license plate as Moroccans in the Sahara are to encounter a Scandinavian blond.

In truth, the United States feels less like a nation than a continent that happens to share a common language and currency. A book that really did justice to all the Highly Individual hotel choices here would rival the Encyclopaedia Britannica. *Hip Hotels USA* can only be a primer, a small glimpse into the experiences that are possible. They include a treehouse fifty feet up a giant cedar in the forests of Washington State, a mid-century modern motel in the Californian desert, a collection of remote lakeside cabins designed by a disciple of Frank Lloyd Wright, and a genteel Florentine palazzo in the rolling farmlands of New England. From coast to coast, from sea to shining sea, these hotel experiences are as diverse as the land itself.

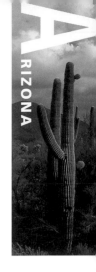
wigwam motel

"Get your kicks…on Route 66." The Rolling Stones helped to make this one of the best-known highways in the world, but the sad fact is that there's not much to sing about now. Winding its way from Albuquerque, New Mexico, to Flagstaff, Arizona, Route 66 has long been upstaged by Interstate 40. You don't even catch a glimpse of Route 66 unless you take an exit and purposely seek it out. And even if you do, it's tough to see where you might get your kicks these days.

The irony is that for decades this was *the* road to opportunity. It was Steinbeck's "Mother Road," the route out of Dust Bowl destitution. Then after the war, thousands of former servicemen migrated west along Route 66 in pursuit of sunshine and opportunity in California. Now all that's left of it is a rusty, dusty ensemble of dented Americana. But that doesn't mean it's not worth a visit. Route 66 today has an eerie, cinematic quality, an atmosphere that only benign neglect can create. Roadside facades could use a lick of paint, some of the buildings are boarded up, and neon signs haven't been maintained so that at night the highway is full of "mo els" and " vice stations." If you are a fan of bizarre road movies à la David Lynch, then Route 66

will appeal. This could be the venue for the next Richard Avedon book, a look at the dusty down-and-out of America; or a Bruce Weber fashion shoot for Russian *Vogue* complete with a posse of six-foot blonde Ukrainian models. Life has passed the old route by – but in some ways that's a blessing. For one thing its soul has not been annihilated by the otherwise unstoppable march of Burger Kings, McDonald's, Dairy Queens, Wendys, Dunkin' Donuts, Subways, Arby's, Taco Bells, Pizza Huts, Chili's, A&Ws, Outback Steakhouses and all the other garish fast-food franchises that dominate American highways.

So there it is – if you want a hundred different ways to increase your cholesterol, don't turn off Interstate 40 to visit Route 66. If, on the other hand, you are fascinated by the decaying B-side of the twentieth-century American dream, then you really must stop at the Wigwam Motel. Driving down Route 66 you can't miss it. The outlines of the white concrete teepees with their graphic red detailing stand out a mile away on this dead flat terrain. When you get closer you realize that the 1950s cars artfully parked outside each wigwam are all part of the show. The Wigwam Motel is more like a permanent highway art installation

posing as a motel, a huge parking-lot size sculpture situated between Route 66 and the old railway tracks.

Now it's time for a confession. Much as I wanted to, I wasn't able to stay the night at the Wigwam Motel. But not for want of trying. I had spent a long day in the car, starting out from Tucson, Arizona, on a long drive that took me through cactus country north of Phoenix to the snow-covered peaks of Flagstaff and on to the high plateau of Navajo County, Arizona, and the town of Holbrook, famous for its petrified fossil forests. I arrived late on a Sunday afternoon, only to discover from a little sign outside the reception hut/souvenir shop that the Wigwam was inexplicably closed that day. Or rather, reception was closed; anyone with keys to one of the freestanding concrete teepees was free to come and go 24/7. But that didn't include me. So close and yet so far. The light and the skies were stunning, however, so I took plenty of pictures and when it got dark I drove back to Interstate 40 and checked in to a brand new and totally uninspiring Holiday Inn. I was scheduled to move on early the next day but my conscience and curiosity wouldn't let me – not without having been inside one of these improbable concrete teepees. So back I drove to good old Route 66. This time I found a janitor happy to show me inside one of the wigwams (I couldn't wait until 3pm, I explained, which is when reception opens during the week). It was comfortable enough, with an ensuite bathroom, a couple of easy chairs, a kingsize bed and a desk – though there was no sign of the old coin-operated radio (the 1950s equivalent of cable TV) whose takings were the original architect's only reimbursement for his work. I was a little disappointed that the rooms did not utilize the full 32-foot ceiling height of the teepee, but it's a minor quibble – no one comes all the way out here for ceiling height, after all. In any case, it was time to go. As I drove away I caught a last glimpse of the sign above the motel that asks "Have you slept in a wigwam lately?" Sadly, not quite.

address Wigwam Motel, 811 West Hopi Drive, Holbrook, Arizona 86025

t +1 (928) 524 3048 **f** +1 (928) 524 9335 **e** clewis97@cybertrails.com

room rates from $35

rancho de la osa

Let's face it, twenty-five years ago if you announced that all you really wanted to do was put on pointy boots, wrangling jeans, a big hat and a western shirt, get on a horse, spit, shout and curse, you would at best have been written off as an overzealous fan of the Village People. But ever since the film *City Slickers* hit theaters in the mid-1990s, it's been (almost) acceptable to admit to fantasies of dressing up and riding out as a cowboy. As we become more affluent, we become more sophisticated, and so escape becomes a more complex issue. It has a psychological aspect as well as geographical one. It's fine to be out of the city, but if all we end up doing is what we do at home – eat, shop, watch television – what's the point of going away at all? Hence the growing appeal of what some people refer to, rather disparagingly, as "theme destinations," but others call adventure retreats. Whatever the terminology, hotels like Rancho de la Osa are the perfect venue for a truly comprehensive escape.

First, in terms of location Rancho de la Osa is exactly where a ranch should be: in the high Sonoran Desert, just a mile from the Mexican border, a land of red earth and canyons once haunted by the likes of Geronimo and Cochise. It's a landscape that evokes every cowboy film

of legend, from *The Magnificent Seven* to *Rio Lobo*. If you take the scenic route to Rancho de la Osa you pass Tombstone, the famous town in Arizona where Doc Holliday faced off at the OK Corral. Thanks to the latitude, the weather is warm and sunny all year round, and apart from the odd US border patrol in a four-wheel drive, there's nobody here – certainly no suburban sprawl to ruin the illusion. Many of the nearby roads are in fact dirt trails that will test the average non-four-wheel drive to its limits. I speak from experience: that hired Corolla will never be the same again after I drove it for the better part of three hours along the dirt road that leads from Nogales to Sasabe, where Rancho de la Osa is located.

This is one of the last great Spanish haciendas in the US. Originally built back in the early 1800s, it has been a guest ranch since the 1920s. But by the time Veronica and Richard Schultz came along, it was in need of work. For these former Flagstaff lawyers, it was a chance to redefine their lives. With bold colors and a careful attention to detail, they have succeeded in converting a moth-balled collection of adobe huts into a Mexican–American melange of vibrant color, eclectic furnishings, and earthy cowboy comforts.

Weathered timber in faded, sunbaked shades adds to Rancho de la Osa's Southwest ambience

Burned-brown walls and simple Mexican furniture make the saloon feel like a cantina straight out of an old Western

Corrugated roofing, cacti, adobe – the architectural aesthetic is part shed, part homestead, part farm

Candy-colored Adirondack chairs in the shade of a veranda provide a place to put your feet up after a ride

Architectural details are executed in Spanish Mission style and the bright color palette of modern Mexico

The vivid blue of the walls surrounding the swimming pool is the same color as Frida Kahlo's Mexico City house

The majority of guestrooms have working fireplaces to take the chill off the desert nights

The paddocks are a reminder that this is a riders' ranch. Guests can lend a hand with tasks like rounding up the cattle

The exterior of the pink John Wayne cottage is a still life of vibrant color and weathered texture

An homage to Frida Kahlo, who helped take the colors of the Mexican village into mainstream culture and beyond

In true American–Mexican tradition, the outdoor fireplace is perfect for enjoying a coffee under the stars

Bleached skulls and colors baked by the Arizona sun – the prevailing aesthetic is Georgia O'Keeffe meets Frida Kahlo

Shaded by gigantic eucalyptus trees, the faded pink walls of the main house come alive in the late-afternoon sun

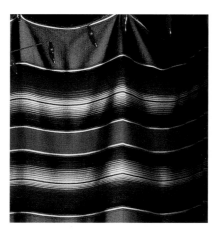

Bright color and quirky details like this traditional Mexican blanket hung up as a curtain epitomize the Rancho's style

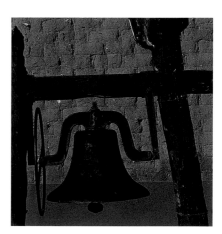

A weather-beaten bronze mission bell summons guests for breakfast, lunch and dinner

In homage to its namesake, the John Wayne cottage is decorated in a style best described as "cozy cowboy"

The colors, textures and shapes are everything we might expect of a ranch in the middle of Papago Indian country

This peaceful room, one of the most secluded in the compound, was John Wayne's favorite

The day here starts with the clanging of the massive bell suspended from a weathered wooden frame outside the old mission building that is now the compound's cantina. The bell is a signal to gather in the communal dining room for breakfast. This is a long room with a fireplace in the middle; food is served on a big refectory table, and everyone eats together – there are no little tables tucked away for romancing couples. Everyone also eats what the kitchen is serving that morning: no à la carte nonsense here. At breakfast a younger version of Curly in *City Slickers* works out the day's "ridin' plan," which often involves rounding up some cattle. Some of the guests have their own boots and hats, but for those who don't the ranch has a supply store that will outfit you. Those not heading out on horseback straight after breakfast are free to swim in the pool that is enclosed in a compound painted the same vibrant indigo blue as Frida Kahlo's famous house in Mexico City. Or they can choose to hang out on the veranda on Adirondack chairs painted in the impossibly bright colors of Mexican village crafts. As it was, I was the only guest who didn't go out riding – much to my disappointment, but I was too busy taking photographs. Still, this gave me the opportunity to explore the many spaces that the Schultzes have created here in the very south of Arizona. Most guestrooms have fireplaces, the furniture is American Southwest in style with lots of Navajo rugs, Mexican antiques, weathered timber, old leather chairs, and painted cupboards, and the walls have the handmade, uneven texture of adobe.

But what's particularly appealing is that aside from all this comfort and style, the Schultzes brought a sense of humor to the design of their Rancho – one look at the bar stools will convince you of that. Even if you don't ride at all – if your fantasy really is more Village People than John Wayne – you can still get in the saddle in the stationary safety of the bar.

---

address   Rancho de la Osa, PO Box 1, Tucson/Sasabe, Arizona 85633

t +1 (520) 823 4257   **f** +1 (520) 823 4238   **e** osagal@aol.com

room rates from $320, including meals and activities

san josé

Austin is the Amsterdam of Texas. It's a relatively small city (by Texan standards), but nevertheless a hive of activity in music, art, theater and literature. It is almost as if all the creative people in this vast state – the second most populous in the union, with 22 million inhabitants – have ended up here. And that despite the fact that Austin is the official state capital, usually the kiss of death for a city's street cred.

The proprietor of the San José comes from a Texas ranching family. But Liz Lambert had long since left and was living and working in New York City as a district attorney when one day, as so often happens to emigrants, she just had to get back home. At the same time the career blues struck: she had to do something other than law. It was time for a change.

Casting about in Austin for opportunities, Lambert discovered that the San José motel was on the market. Located on South Congress, a broad avenue leading to the city's Washington DC-like capitol building, it had originally opened in 1936 as the San José "motor court," offering carpeted comfort and individual garages – the height of modernity. By 1995, it was still a motel, but only just. The place had followed the general decline into seediness

and neglect that had afflicted the whole of downtown Austin. What had been the city's premier motel was now a rent-by-the-hour haunt of addicts and prostitutes.

All Lambert's years of arguing her case in court didn't enable her to win over her banker to her vision of converting the San José to a fashionable hotel; ditto for most of the other banks she went to see. So for the first few years she ran the place as it was. But eventually she did raise the money and in 1998 the San José closed for a total renovation. Despite knowing nothing about the hotel business, as she freely admits, Lambert was now very much in the hotel business.

Playing slum landlord and madam for a couple of years was perhaps a good thing, for it clearly gave Lambert the time to reflect on how best to tackle the renovation of the San José. Architecturally speaking, the result is such a successful reinvention of the American motel that I'm convinced it will become the model for low-rise accommodation throughout the United States. Lambert and her architect Bob Harris, of the architectural firm Lake/Flato, took a property consisting of semi-detached bungalows with parking spaces out front, removed the car spaces and the car access,

and replaced them with an intricate maze of cactus-lined paths and alleys, mini-courtyards, pergolas, potted plants, and bamboo screens. This dovetailing of landscaping and architecture magnifies both the sense of green and the sense of privacy, and it adds up to a spatial sophistication that both intrigues and soothes. There's still space to park, but your car no longer takes pride of place – the parking lot is separate from the complex, which is as it should be.

The interiors are stylishly simple, an appropriate contrast to the complex collection of outdoor spaces. The studio-like guestrooms have polished concrete floors and white-tiled bathrooms, and fans of the minimalist artist Donald Judd will recognize his influence in the timber furniture, made from reclaimed 1930s pine. The new San José strikes a perfect balance between privacy and conviviality. Your bungalow is secluded enough to function as an urban retreat; but should you be gripped by the desire to be in the thick of things, you only need

wander over to the outdoor bar surrounding the bamboo-enclosed pool. It hasn't taken long for the San José to become one of the best places to hang out in Austin, and the likes of kd lang and Sandra Bullock count it among their favorite hotels. The atmosphere is so relaxed that many people who turn up for a drink end up staying into the small hours. Even in winter the courtyard is busy, with an enormous cast-iron kettle hosting a big fire, and a series of outdoor heaters to take the bite out of the evening chill.

As befits a place where design has been integrated into every detail, breakfast arrives in a generous custom-made bento box. Though there's no restaurant on the premises, Güero's, one of Austin's best restaurants, is just up the road and the city's premier live music venue, the Continental Club, is right across the street. Indeed, the downtown neighborhood of Austin has undergone a grassroots revival that has lined its streets with antique shops, cozy cafés and lively bars. Just, in fact, like Amsterdam.

---

address Hotel San José, 1316 South Congress, Austin, Texas 78704

t +1 (512) 444 7322 **f** +1 (512) 444 7362 **e** reservations@sanjosehotel.com

room rates from $125

xv beacon

If there's a dominant image of Boston, then it's got to be Ally McBeal. I know it's no longer on the air, but I ask you, what other show, or film for that matter, has ever made life in a city look so much fun? Where else could there be a thriving law practice consisting exclusively of good-looking partners who have their own bar/nightclub downstairs? Even winter looked appealing on Ally McBeal – all snowflakes and Christmas carols outside, and cozy bars with live music inside.

OK, OK it was all make-believe, but even if there's no Ally in real life, there is an area in Boston called Beacon Hill, where the show was set and filmed. Flanked by the Boston Common and the Boston Public Garden, and around the corner from the State House, Beacon Hill has long been the city's most desirable location. The neighborhood has a substantial heritage – this is where Boston's first resident, the Reverend William Blaxton, settled in 1622. But today's Beacon Hill is a far cry from the Puritan ethos of the city's stern founders. It is an atmospheric mix of boutiques, antique shops, historic townhouses and fashionable restaurants. And these days there's an air of youthful success to the place, and an affluence firmly rooted in the new, digital economy.

Until the opening of XV Beacon, there was nowhere in Boston that catered to this new generation of entrepreneurs. (Not 15, mind, but XV – the figures that are carved into the building's handsome stone facade and somehow capture the character of this small but immaculately luxurious hotel.) "XV Beacon," says proprietor Paul G. Roiff, "is tailored to a class of executive whose way of life couldn't have been imagined by the people who built Boston's older hotels. When I think of the Ritz I think of my grandparents. When I think of the Four Seasons I think of my parents." No prizes for guessing who comes to mind when he thinks of his own hotel. But this was a project that soon developed its own momentum. "It started out as one thing," says Roiff, "but then we got carried away and it became much more extravagant." That's certainly true: the wine cellar alone is reputed to have cost $4.5 million and among its 30,000-odd bottles are some $12,000 bottles of 1907 Heidsieck Monopole champagne rescued from the hold of a sunken schooner at the bottom of the Baltic.

But whatever the titillating statistics of the wine cellar, the real attraction is the interiors. Despite being in the very heart of New England, there was one thing Roiff was certain of: he did not want Chippendale and chintz. Instead he called in Celeste Cooper, one of Boston's big names in interior design, known for her knack of juxtaposing old and new to create an ambience that is both austere and romantic. Despite the seeming contradiction, she pulled it off. XV Beacon has a kind of groovy Patrician aesthetic, a traditional New England style with a minimalist twist. This is not a hotel afraid to abandon pink and apricot, opting instead for a sophisticated and admittedly masculine color palette of cream, cocoa, espresso, cappuccino, and all those other trendy words for rich shades of brown. Rooms all have an open fire, but the fireplaces are anything but traditional, set in a panel of gleaming stainless steel, which in turn is set in a cocoa-stained paneled wall. Such is the decorative rhythm of XV Beacon that for every traditional touch – an antique mahogany side table, for instance – there's a thoroughly contemporary counterpoint such as a polished aluminium bowl filled with tangerines. And in contrast to the imposing historic exterior, the interior features a significant collection of modern art. Original works include *Green Dot*, an oil painting by abstractionist Jules Olitski in the lobby, two Gilbert Stuarts in the Federalist restaurant and two pieces by Theodoros Stamos in the dining room. With Kiehl's products in the bathroom, mini-bars stocked with Ketel One vodka and Krug champagne, a fleet of three chauffered S500 Mercedes Sedans, antique canopied beds in the guestrooms, and one of New England's best chefs in the kitchen, XV Beacon has overlooked nothing in its ambition to cater to the next generation of well-to-do hotel customers.

If anything it's almost over the top. Take Cindy Selby, executive pastry chef at the Fed. Aside from being responsible for the restaurant's excellent desserts, the most Boston moment on her CV is the fact that the Phoenix Art Museum presented her with an award for "edible architecture" – for her chocolate and cast sugar replica of the Louvre. Ally herself would have been proud.

address XV Beacon, 15 Beacon Street, Boston, Massachusetts 02108-2902

t +1 (617) 670 1500 **f** +1 (617) 670 2525 **e** hotel@xvbeacon.com

room rates from $295

duchamp

By the standards of the usual Sonoma or Napa Valley hotel or bed and breakfast, Duchamp is a real oddity. No chintz, no antiques, no cozy curtains…what kind of country hotel is this? But given that it was named in honor of the Surrealist Marcel Duchamp, you don't need to see it to guess that it is no ordinary hotel. Pat Lenz, sculptor and the visual impresario behind Duchamp, is candid: "There's no way I could live in a Laura Ashley, potpourri-filled place. I'd rather see nothing than a whole lot of stuff." And indeed, Duchamp is sleek, modern and clutter free. But eliminating clutter was by no means the only premise here. Pat and Peter Lenz, no strangers to the hospitality industry, having successfully operated a restaurant and winery in the Hamptons, started by posing a simple question. Why do people from the city (San Francisco, Oakland, Palo Alto) make the trek to Napa or Sonoma Valley? The obvious answer is to visit the wineries. But the deeper reason is surely the urge to escape the city environment, to get some breathing room. So the Lenzes set out to create a retreat, a place of calm, privacy and beauty.

This transplanted East Coast couple found what they were looking for in sleepy Healdsburg, an old-fashioned Sonoma Valley town some sixty-five miles north of San Francisco. Back then the site consisted of a metal shed and some derelict shacks a block away from the town square – only the optimistic imagination of an artistically minded couple could possibly have recognized it as an opportunity for a hotel. But if their plans seemed a little surreal to locals, they knew exactly what they wanted to create. Their vision was of a modern but mellow luxury lodging, a self-contained cluster of cottages in which guests could discover a profound sense of tranquillity.

The first task was to gut and rebuild all the original sheds and shacks. Each one was then furnished and designed in homage to one of Pat Lenz's favorite twentieth-century artists. Hence the Duchamp Hotel has cottages dedicated to Miro, Man Ray, Warhol and Picasso. In the Man Ray cottage, red neon lips glow above a modern fireplace. The Picasso house has more of a farmhouse feel, with cowskin rugs and a driftwood nude. The Warhol cottage is all-white with just a splash of red and a couple of Marilyn posters. In addition, the Lenzes built six new one-bedroom villas in which each and every detail was designed to make them the ultimate chill-out cabins.

D.a.D.A

The steel-blue skies, unrelenting sunshine
and occasional eucalyptus
are California at its best

Each guest cabin is like a mini-loft – a
pristine, clutter-free base from which to
explore the Napa and Sonoma Valleys

A lot of care went into creating
Duchamp's carefree atmosphere.
Every detail is deliberate

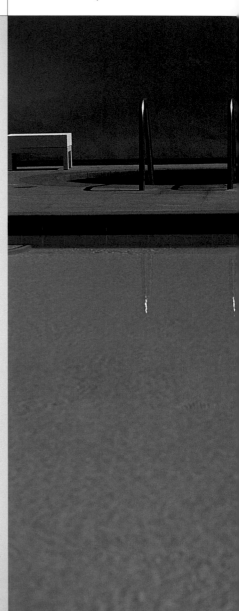

The enormous bathrooms feature a
runway length of stainless steel counter
and a shower large enough for a horse

Texture and color are provided by
details like this Burmese bronze tabouret
and bright yellow wall light (below left)

Interiors inspired by the art of Donald
Judd combine the simplicity of concrete,
linen and wood with the luxury of space

They are square in form, with polished concrete floors, tin roofs and an interior that reflects a sculptor's disciplined linear sense; all the headboards, desks and daybeds are at exactly the same height. Pat Lenz herself painstakingly mapped out every detail and then called in an architect to make her design a reality.

None of this premeditation is evident when you arrive at Duchamp. Quite the opposite, in fact. The place feels decidedly laid-back, with a very laissez-faire attitude. There might be the odd guest taking a morning swim in the elegant granite-lined pool, or a couple lingering in the shed over a breakfast of strong coffee and pastries from the local bakery. Judging from the utter tranquillity, I suspect many guests don't actually make it to the wineries at all.

In an impressionistic way, the place reminds me very much of Australia. It's not just the warm climate under a steel-blue sky; but the palette of materials is also characteristically antipodean − painted plywood, corrugated iron, tin roofs, not to mention the odd eucalyptus

tree about the site. But there's nowhere in the Australian outback offering this standard of accommodation. The new villas in particular are extremely refined pieces of interior architecture. From the simple timber furniture inspired by the work of Donald Judd, to the huge bathrooms with their runway stretches of pressed stainless steel, there are few places in even the world's biggest cities that come up to these design standards.

And that's the point of Duchamp Hotel − it was created for people every bit as design conscious as the Lenzes themselves. It is an example of a growing phenomenon in the world of highly individual hotels: the conviction that if you create a place in the image of where you yourself would like to spend time, there will be people out there who share your taste. It's a new approach to marketing. Instead of "give the people what they want," it's "give the people what you want." As Duchamp himself is reputed to have said, "It's art if the artist says it is." Quite!

---

address Duchamp Hotel, 421 Foss Street, Healdsburg, California 95448

t +1 (707) 431 1300 **f** +1 (707) 431 1333 **e** info@duchamphotel.com

room rates from $225

post ranch inn

Situated between Carmel (former mayor, Clint Eastwood) and San Simeon (location of Hearst Castle), the Post Ranch Inn is on the most picturesque stretch of highway in the USA. Highway 1 is possibly the most famous road in the nation, and this is the portion that earned its reputation. North of Carmel the coast flattens out, and south of San Simeon the landscape has been invaded by the suburban towns that keep creeping ever further beyond Los Angeles. But in between, winding its way along the most dramatic cliffs, beaches and ridges of America's Pacific coast, this single-lane strip of Highway 1 is still like the movies – a fantasy road straight out of the Beach Boys' "Surfing USA."

Post Ranch Inn itself is easily the most spectacularly situated hotel in the USA, perched as it is on a ridge that drops several thousand feet down to the azure lapping waves of the Pacific. In fact the connotations of the name are pretty misleading. The word ranch usually suggests flat grazing land, while the word post conjures a rustic homestead with a porch and lots of gingham. Neither could be further from the truth. The landscape here is anything but flat and gentle, and there is nothing remotely nostalgic or rustic about the architecture. In fact

the place is named after the Post family, who have maintained a homestead here since 1850. But this is definitely not a dude ranch. It's a place where the architecture is as adventurous as the location. Arriving at Post Ranch is pure theater. You approach along a small mountain road that winds its way through dense forest and past distant craggy granite peaks, until you arrive at reception, a stylish ultra-modern A-frame at the base of a heavily wooded ridge. At this point no other part of the complex has yet revealed itself, but before you can go any further you must park and transfer to a courtesy car to be driven up the final ridge. Nothing can prepare you for the spectacle that reveals itself when you do finally climb the crest. Arranged along an impossibly thin ribbon of paved path are a series of treehouses and ocean cottages that gaze across a vast expanse of nothing but sea and sky. The land drops away steeply, cliff-like, to the Pacific below. The courtesy vehicles not only save guests the hazard of driving along such a precarious and unfamiliar ridge, they also fuel a sense of anticipation that is part of a perfectly orchestrated experience.

But if the most stunning feature of Post Ranch is the setting, the manmade contribution is not far behind. Hidden among the trees on

the high side of the ridge are the treehouses. Suspended on timber stilts, these are a melange of triangular shapes creating an interior unlike any other. Each corner of the triangular bed-living-room is a transparent glass angle – one housing a triangular desk, one a triangular daybed, and the last a triangular fireplace with a glass back wall. The partly glazed ceiling rises to a peak, forming another triangle and giving extraordinary height to the space.

The ocean houses are similarly innovative, albeit in a completely different fashion. These are camouflaged not by trees but by being virtually buried in the side of the steep slope from which they look out. The roofs are covered in topsoil and planted – so effective is the disguise that there are signs imploring guests not to walk there. In contrast to the triangular treehouses, the ocean houses are a complex ensemble of curved lines intersected by curved chimneys and immense stretches of glass.

It was no surprise to discover that the architect of Post Ranch Inn, Mickey Muennig,

was strongly influenced by the work of Frank Lloyd Wright. Muennig studied with Bruce Goff at the University of Oklahoma, where he developed a humanistic approach to his craft. His fusion of glass, stone, slate and native woods reflects a lifelong commitment to environmentally appropriate design.

Extraordinary location, extraordinary architecture – but even these are not the only drawing cards of Post Ranch Inn. Because many guests come first and foremost for the food. Chef Craig Von Foerster's new California cuisine is truly world-class. Even so, architecturally speaking the Sierra Mar restaurant is another tour de force, combining rugged timber and immense stretches of floor-to-ceiling glass that afford magnificent views of the Pacific Ocean.

As the suburban sprawl continues its march north of Santa Barbara and south of Palo Alto, each year there's less and less wilderness along Pacific Highway 1. Post Ranch Inn is a small, refined slice of how it all could or should have been.

address Post Ranch Inn at Big Sur, Highway 1, PO Box 219, Big Sur, California 93920

t +1 (831) 667 2200 **f** +1 (831) 667 2824 **e** info@postranchinn.com

room rates from $485

the intercontinental

Downtown Gotham – if there's a hotel anywhere in the US that could work as a ready-made Batman filmset, it would be this Chicago skyscraper. At the top it's all gargoyles and turrets and spires – perfect for hanging from a bat rope. Inside the gothic detailing continues with stone balls, coffered ceilings, punctured metal wall lamps, heavy oak tables, stone floors and bronze relief elevator doors – a collection of public spaces that is eclectic beyond imagination. There's a ballroom inspired by the Knights of the Round Table; a Louis XIV, chateau-like meeting room with soaring ceilings, tapestries and chandeliers; an Assyrian Hall of Lions complete with two marble lions; an Art Deco lobby; a neo-gothic lobby; a Spanish Mission-inspired lobby with a fountain topped by a stone replica of King Solomon's head…and the list goes on.

Stop right there, you may be thinking – this all sounds a bit too Disneyland for my liking. But improbable as it may seem, all these themed rooms are definitely not unattractive. Perhaps it's because they were all created in the 1920s, making them now virtually antique, particularly by American standards. Besides, a folly is almost always entertaining. And the most extravagant folly of all in what is quite a

collection of bizarre architectural outings is the hotel's pool. Situated between the eleventh and twelfth floors, this is not what you expect to find half-way up a skyscraper, particularly a skyscraper of this vintage. Yet there it is, a 25-meter giant – half Olympic size no less, set in a soaring space and flanked by elaborate walls of leaded glass rising to the substantial ceiling height. On first impression, this is not a swimming pool, it's a cathedral filled with water, and even after eighty years it's the swimming pool that remains the hotel's star attraction. People often inquire if the pool is still open before they make a reservation.

So what's the story? How did all this Gotham-like exotica come about? It started with a group of successful businessmen in Chicago between the wars. Having achieved the American dream of success, money and fame, they decided to build the ultimate athletic club, the best in the country, bar none. And it was to be in a building the likes of which the city had never seen before. That's how such a spectacular Florentine-style piece of aquatic sculpture ended up on the twelfth floor. Originally there was also an archery range, running track, bowling alley, golf driving range and gymnasium. But these were giddy days –

the Medinah Athletic Club opened its doors in 1929, and shut them again in 1934, one more victim of the catastrophic Wall Street Crash.

Times change, and gothic lobbies and church-like swimming pools are not enough to entice today's business traveller. So when the Intercontinental group acquired the building in 1988, they embarked on a quarter-billion dollar restoration program that not only recreated the original designs in authentic detail, but also laid on cable TV, internet access and all the other high-tech extras demanded by today's traveler. So much is only to be expected of a business hotel; less predictable was to open a series of trend-setting bars and restaurants that have become favorites in Chicago among people who wear Prada. For lots of different reasons, the Intercontinental Chicago has become a focal point in the city. There are weddings in the King Arthur Foyer, annual general meetings in the Louis XIV room, children who can't wait to drag their parents to that pool, and people meeting for lunch and

dinner in the Zest restaurant. It's become a small world of its own, with a constant flow of people coming in, going out, running to functions, hurrying to lunch or a meeting – a hive of activity with a real buzz. And that's the fun of it. Where else might you come across, as I did, a parade of 120 people all identically dressed in cut-off denim shorts and yellow T-shirts bearing the words "2002 family reunion cousin no. X"?

The Intercontinental Chicago is a hodgepodge, an oddball collection of some very avant-garde design, complete with fiber optics and asymmetrical custom-designed contemporary furniture; a very businesslike lobby with lots of bronze urns, a sparkling onyx and marble mosaic-tiled floor, and people in dark suits; and then all those Batman bits where groups straight out of *My Big Fat Greek Wedding* are holding family celebrations. Brash, extravagant, eccentric – it will never win any awards for streamlining, but who cares when it's so much fun to stay there?

address Intercontinental Chicago, 505 North Michigan Avenue, Chicago, Illinois 60611

t +1 (312) 944 4100   **f** +1 (312) 944 1320   **e** chicago@interconti.com

room rates from $209

the peninsula

The relationship between Chicago's Intercontinental and Peninsula hotels reminds me of my parents' families. My father, one of seven children, came from a household where there was always noise. A lot of noise. At dinner everyone spoke at the same time, and the whole event would last hours because my grandmother – not the greatest of cooks – could never manage to get more than one dish on the table at a time. The age difference between eldest and youngest meant that while some of the children were talking grown-up subjects, others were still disappearing under the big old oak table to tie everyone's shoelaces together. In short it was chaos, and my mother loved it. In her family, dinner without the proper silver and crystal was unthinkable. Form was insisted upon, right down to the chilled butterballs in their own crystal dish. My surgeon grandfather, who had usually spent the day covered in blood, preferred to dine in silence unless someone could offer morsels of information about wine or interior design, his two passions. When my father and mother met, she always wanted to eat at his house, because it was such a mad free-for-all, and he wanted to go to her place, because it was so civilized.

Well if the Intercontinental is my father's parents' place, the Peninsula is my mother's. One is crazy and chaotic, but a whole lot of fun; the other is chic, elegant and subdued. Anyone who has ever stayed in the Hong Kong Peninsula will know what extraordinarily high standards of service and aesthetics are set there. As a benchmark, it was insanely ambitious, and frankly there were a lot of shaking heads when the Peninsula Group first announced that it was to open in the American Midwest. The USA is not Asia, skeptics said; such a standard of service is almost impossible to attain, let alone maintain. But the people at Peninsula were undaunted, and the group went ahead and embarked on the creation of a new Chicago landmark.

The result is possibly the most genteel hotel in the entire United States. As in its Hong Kong namesake, the rooms are large and luxuriously appointed, with Sony widescreen televisions, two-line telephones, personal fax machines, and high-speed internet access, as well as exquisite marble bathrooms, down pillows, luxurious bedlinen, understated furniture, and soft amber lighting. So far, so good. There is also an amazing spa, as in Hong Kong, that most guests find hard to leave.

There's a beautiful aqua mosaic-tiled pool, flanked by floor-to-ceiling windows, on the twentieth floor. The view is straight out to the shores of Lake Michigan (which are skipping distance from the hotel). For those with the time (and you should really make the time) the spa has a whirlpool and lap pool, gym, yoga room and steam room, and any number of oriental treatments to make you feel like you have been to Hong Kong, even if you never have.

In so many respects – the view, the restrained luxury, the army of staff on hand to attend to your every whim, the gilded Asia-meets-Art-Deco style – the Hong Kong Peninsula and the Chicago Peninsula are a lot alike. Even the neighborhoods they inhabit offer similarly world-class shopping. Admittedly there's scarcely anywhere in the world to beat Hong Kong for shopping, but as far as the US is concerned, Chicago is not far behind New York. And when it comes to convenience, the Peninsula probably beats any hotel in the Big Apple: almost all the stores worth going to are no more than a mile from the hotel. From big-name department stores to the smallest boutiques, they are all in the zone known as the Magnificent Mile, an eight-block stretch of style and couture that takes in boutique-lined Oak Street and runs into Michigan Avenue and up to the lake. There's also plenty of culture to divert you in Chicago: you could take a tour of Frank Lloyd Wright's architectural legacy, or you could make time to visit the Art Institute of Chicago.

But my hunch is that you will almost certainly be too busy indulging yourself. It is remarkable how the Chicago Peninsula has managed to recreate the experience of staying in the Hong Kong Peninsula. It's all about dressing up in your best clothes for dinner, ordering late-night snacks with champagne, recovering in the spa, and hitting the town feeling like a million bucks. There aren't many hotels in the world that can create that feeling. I think they even do butterballs in crystal dishes.

---

address The Peninsula Chicago, 108 East Superior Street, Chicago, Illinois 60611

t +1 (312) 337 2888 **f** +1 (312) 751 2888 **e** pch@peninsula.com

room rates from $445

the townhouse

It's hard to believe, but Miami's South Beach is still changing. Anyone who was here five years ago would have witnessed the full thrust of its real estate rebirth. Every Art Deco building was being restored and every other marginally worthwhile building was being converted into a restaurant, boutique or bar. The question was, where would it stop? Just how many fashionable hotels and restaurants could South Beach possibly accommodate?

Five years on the answer is clear…a lot! Back then most of the renovation activity was centered on Ocean Drive and a few streets back from it. The area around Collins Avenue on the other side of Lincoln Road remained largely untouched. With the exception of the Delano, this was the Miami of old: cheap diners, boarded-up buildings, and lots of retirees in checkered shorts and golf caps. Today the shorts, the diners and the dereliction have disappeared. In their place are restaurants, boutiques, hotels and yet more shops dedicated to sunglasses. South Beach has secured its status as *the* warm weather destination for the urban all-night party with a Latin twist, and the appeal only seems to increase as its critical mass grows.

Almost unimaginably amid such a plethora of hotels, there was still a gap in the market, a gap plugged very convincingly by the seventy-room Townhouse, described as a place for people with more style than money. Now usually (with the exception of the Standard) the "more dash, less cash line" leaves me skeptical. Less cash almost always means less dash, especially in big cities. But the Townhouse pulls it off – partly because of its location, partly because of the laid-back, entertaining nature of its design. Situated right on the beach, a stone's throw from the Delano and next door to the pristine but much pricier Shore Club, the Townhouse has a location you would expect to be much more expensive. And what Paris-based interior designer India Mahdavi did with the site is interesting, irrespective of budget. Her starting point was a basic white-on-white approach – not particularly original, given that Starck did this for the Delano more than a decade ago. But it is only a starting point. In the bedroom, spaces are jazzed up with circular rugs in fire-engine red or pale blue, and a touch of coziness is added by a rectangular lamp in a typically English pink chintz. The rooms avoid hospital-style sterility (often a complaint at the Delano) with other simple touches such as a big beach ball on the bed and a red Batman phone.

The camp 1960s phone looks like
Batman's hotline to the mayor
of Gotham City

Designer India Mahdavi introduced pink
English chintz to counter the austerity
of so much hospital-issue white

The Townhouse's bold red and white
logo appears on everything from
water bottles to matchboxes

TOW

ET MIAMI BEACH FL 331

White is right. It's nothing new, but it works perfectly with Miami's laid-back atmosphere and sweltering weather

Arranged to feel like a family dining room, the breakfast corner has the odd artful splash of red

Details like the beachball and chintz hanging lamp make all-white rooms more playground, less sanitarium

NHŌ
MIAMI

In the lobby the same splashes of fire-engine red and pink chintz create a similar effect, as does the introduction of slightly mismatched furniture. The ingredients are plain but the effect is fun and stylish. The idea, says Mahdavi, was to create an unpretentious place whose keyword was "happy." It might sound naive, but it's true – the Townhouse really is a fun hotel with an upbeat vibe. That's what makes it work.

There are some aspects of Mahdavi's inventive design that certainly are original in Miami. There's no pool, for instance, but that has been changed into a plus by turning the roof into an outdoor living room lined with vast red waterbeds for reclining. Perhaps more than anything else, what makes the Townhouse is attitude. Guestrooms have a couch that can easily accommodate an extra friend (at no extra charge), there are exercise machines in the corridors, the downstairs lounge serves sushi and cocktails, there are puzzles and board games in the lobby and the rooftop hosts a real party scene. It's a cool place to chill out cheaply.

India Mahdavi began her career in the studios of Christian Liaigre, a designer acknowledged for his fine eye and corresponding prices. Since then her work has included the redesign of a large property for English Heritage, and the company headquarters for upscale fashion retailer Joseph. So she was never an obvious choice to steer a budget project. But Jonathan Morr, dynamic proprietor of the Townhouse, welcomed the chance to work with her. "It would have been easy to go with a big-name designer," he shrugs, "but it's more interesting to work with someone who has untapped potential."

Morr has unusual attitudes when it comes to the business of bars, restaurants and hotels. He is not for instance a fan of the celebrity system (invite the celebrities and the rest will come); in fact he prefers the more elusive strategy of not telling anyone where your place is. In short, he's a bit of a character, and in the Townhouse, it shows.

address The Townhouse Hotel, 150 20th Street (at Collins Avenue), Miami Beach, Florida 33139

t +1 (305) 534 3800 **f** +1 (305) 534 3811 **e** info@townhousehotel.com

room rates from $115

the raleigh

This is *the* pool – immortalized in the movies of synchronized swimmer Esther Williams, voted by *Travel & Leisure* magazine as one of the ten most beautiful in the world, lauded by *Life* in the fifties as the most glamorous swimming pool in Florida, this giant pastiche of baroque curves surrounded by Moroccan medjul palm trees can still, more than six decades later, elicit oohs and ahs from new guests. There are larger pools in Miami, some with fountains in the middle, but none has the sensational impact of the Raleigh's jewel-like Art Deco lagoon.

Designed and built in 1940 at the peak of Miami's formative years, the Raleigh is one of architect Lawrence Murray Dixon's mature works. Dixon, recently the subject of a major retrospective at the Bass Museum of Art, was the most prolific and acclaimed architect of Miami Beach during the 1930s and '40s. As the designer of the Tides, the Marlin, the Atlantis and numerous other hotels and apartment buildings, Dixon is credited with bringing Art Deco to Miami. This part of the city has been listed in its entirety on the National Register of Historic Buildings.

What distinguishes Dixon's legacy above all is the way that he reinvented the Art Deco style to suit Miami's emergence as the pre-eminent resort destination in the United States in the 1920s and '30s. In the earliest days of Miami's transformation from a sub-tropical barrier island, developers, engineers and entrepreneurs were more interested in making the fledgling city pseudo-Mediterranean. The first grand hotels were built in the elaborate and hugely expensive manner of the properties of Nice and Cannes – because Miami had been pegged as a rich man's playground, this was the architectural style assumed to be appropriate. But the Mediterranean Revival came to an abrupt end with the stock market crash of 1929. It was during the post-Depression 1930s that Miami Beach acquired the iconic style for which it is renowned today. Tourism for the middle classes, not just the rich, was the new popular dream of the 1930s, and Miami was not only the fastest growing city in the United States, but its architects were inventing a new aesthetic to embody that dream. They ditched the lavish and anachronistic Mediterranean idiom in favor of streamlined Art Deco.

This was a style that was unequivocally oriented to the future. It celebrated the industrial age with a visual vocabulary that borrowed heavily from the great ocean liners of the era: buildings had masts, polished metal surfaces, shiny glass, and exterior trim lines in bright greens, blues, oranges or pinks set against huge expanses of neutral white or beige, echoing the hull of a ship. It was a style disciplined by the constraints of budget, and the Art Deco buildings of South Beach are essentially fairly simple box-like structures. But they are saved from the banality of their uniform geometry by flamboyant ornamental flourishes, an adornment that came to express the fantasy of Florida. Pelicans, tropical fish, serpents and palm trees were incorporated into stylized sculptural friezes along the exterior of many buildings. Inside, it became practically inconceivable by the mid-1930s for a hotel not to have murals. These featured everything from a Native American paddling his canoe through the Florida Everglades to dancing figures frolicking on a beach to wild geese and pink flamingos lifting into flight beneath a silver ceiling: the visual themes captured the escapist fantasy that Miami represented in the national imagination.

Among the many architectural treasures that have survived from Miami's golden age, the Raleigh has always been able to claim the best bones. So it's highly appropriate that this most South Beach of all South Beach hotels should have fallen into the capable hands of André Balazs. As proprietor and impresario of some of America's most individual hotels, Balazs is famous for his ability to make a place hip. His flair is not just for creating surface style, but also for pinpointing and amplifying the essence of what makes a particular place unique. The Mercer is SoHo to the core, Chateau Marmont is as LA as it gets, and now Balazs is pulling off the same feat with Miami's legendary Raleigh. Art Deco was never just about seductive show, it was also about the art of living, and it's this dual philosophy that Balazs has brought to the renovation of the Raleigh. The result is neither loud nor flashy, but memorable in a more subtle way – like an exquisitely tailored suit, whose quality, originality and impeccable taste reveal themselves without the need for fanfare.

address The Raleigh Hotel, South Beach, Ocean Front at 1775 Collins Avenue, Miami Beach, Florida 33139

t +1 (305) 534 6300 **f** +1 (305) 538 8140 **e** reservations@raleighhotel.com

room rates from $275

hotel derek

Independent, adventurous, unpredictable, rich, powerful, patriotic, wild – the city of Houston has a lot in common with its namesake Sam Houston, one of the great figures in Texan history. This pioneer from Tennessee was a famously tough and rugged individualist who lived for some years among the Cherokee Indians and spoke their language fluently. In 1836 Houston led a ragtag band of men to a brilliant victory against the Mexican forces of Santa Anna and went on to become president of the independent republic of Texas.

Houston, the fourth largest city in the United States, deserves to bear his name. It is a city unlike any other. First, this oil city is the city of the car, even more so than Los Angeles. Life without one is unthinkable. It's also a city without any zoning or planning. Texans like their freedom, and that includes being able to build what they want where they want. For the first-time visitor it's all a bit confusing. Factories, office buildings, shopping centers and exclusive residential areas are mixed together in a manner that only a Texan can make sense of. Hotel Derek is a good example. My first thought on arriving was "nice hotel, pity it's not in the city." From my bedroom I could see the towers of downtown Houston off

in the distance. Only later did I discover that as far as Houston society is concerned, this *is* the center of the city. Downtown, Houstonians will tell you, is only for working. When it comes to the city's favorite pastime of spending money (don't forget Enron was a Houston-based company) the Derek is the place to be. Directly opposite is the Galleria shopping center, one of the world's biggest malls. Here there are more designer boutiques and upscale department stores than on New York's Fifth Avenue, all of it air-conditioned and surrounded by a sea of parking spaces.

The Galleria is the focal point for an excess that is characteristically Houstonian. Sam Houston himself, besides being a tough commander, was a bit of a dandy. When he worked as an Indian agent, he would turn up in Washington dressed as a Cherokee chief. Later, as commander of the first Texan army, he commissioned the most elaborate uniforms for himself. In keeping with such precedents, modern Houston hostess Becca Cason Thrash is known as Tri-Becca because she changes at least three times in the course of her parties. For one of her recent bashes, she imported a gondola from Venice to dress up her pool. This is Texas, after all, unashamedly bold and brash.

If they haven't got it in Houston, they'll buy it and ship it in. That's how the city got a resident opera, ballet, symphony orchestra and several theater companies. There's also the Menil Collection, featuring some of the finest artworks of the twentieth century in a gallery designed by Renzo Piano. But the "Hall of Fame Excess Award" has to go to 1960s hostess Joanne King Herring who to complete the ambience of her Roman toga party hired a troop of black Boy Scouts to dress as Nubian slaves.

Until recently the only thing missing from the social hub of Houston was a hotel with a contemporary edge. Enter the Derek. Housed in a nondescript glass tower of the kind that is littered throughout the vast area that comprises Greater Houston, it's the accommodation counterpart to the mall it faces: not much to look at from the outside, but sumptuously and interestingly executed inside. The design signature, like that of Houstonians themselves, is conservatively trendy. Bathrooms are all white, stainless steel, and glass; bedside lamps are made from perforated chromed steel; bedheads are in a darkish timber; and the daybed sits along the length of windows that extend the full width and height of the wall.

Yet there is something authentically Texan about this contemporary hotel. In a state where everything is larger than life, what really sets the Derek apart is space. Corridors are broad, rooms are big, the lobby is bigger, and you can always find a private corner all to yourself. Then there is the huge all-black stretch Yukon they send to fetch you from the airport. This is very much a Texas car – it no doubt does a fraction of a mile to the gallon, but it's a lot more macho than a stretch limo. Where it matters, however, the Derek is decidedly un-Texan – although it has 314 rooms, it still feels like a small and intimate hotel, thanks largely to designer Dayna Lee's clever arrangement that tucks meeting rooms and conference areas out of sight. Houston is a city that will undoubtedly grow on you – just don't plan to walk anywhere.

address Hotel Derek, 2525 West Loop South, Houston, Texas 77027

t +1 (713) 961 3000 **f** +1 (713) 297 4392 **e** derek@hotelderek.com

room rates from $245

avalon

By Hollywood standards the Avalon has some real history. Back when it was still the Beverly Carlton, Marilyn Monroe lived here for two years. And the hotel's reception area was regularly featured in *I Love Lucy*.

Design-wise, the greatest achievement of Avalon Hotel today is that it creates the impression that little has changed. It feels like a well-preserved gem, a 1950s building that has been beautifully maintained. The reality couldn't be further from the truth. The mid-century vision of pristine design that greets the visitor was in fact constructed practically from scratch. When Brad Korzen, a Chicago native who made his fortune developing commercial properties, decided to turn his hand to hotels, the Avalon was a prime property only in terms of its potential. Korzen deserves credit for assembling such an interesting team to achieve such a seamless result.

The restoration process started with some research. Interior designer Kelly Wearstler found and studied photographs of the property by legendary West Coast photographer Julius Shulman. But they revealed little she could work with. So to tackle the spatial complexities she approached transplanted Aussie architects Henk Koning and Julie Eizenberg. They instituted major changes which, to their credit, today seem completely natural. The hotel consists of three buildings: the Olympic Building of 1949, the Beverly Building of 1953, and the Canon built in 1962. When you enter the hotel you are confronted by a sweeping view of the original hour-glass shaped pool and the row of cabana spaces that open onto it. What you would never guess is that this spatial transparency is entirely new. The elevator and its shaft used to stand directly opposite the entrance, blocking the interior view. Koning Eizenberg's bold proposal was to move the entire elevator and place it in a newly designed tower added on to the rear side of the building, an avant-garde structure clad in copper that Eizenberg calls her "fat Brancusi" after its resemblance to the sculptor's famous geometric totems. Other structural changes included moving walls to expand the lobby and restaurant spaces. Finally, the facade was reinvented with a striking basketweave pattern executed in mosaic tiles.

Inside, Kelly Wearstler's design succeeds by seamlessly blending the old with the new. It was never her intention to mindlessly mimic 1950s style, but to create an exciting contemporary space that would evoke the mid-century spirit.

Avalon's architects Koning Eizenberg created extra lobby space by putting the elevator in this copper-clad tower

Design classics combine with custom-made pieces to evoke the mid-century spirit without slavish imitation

The aqua color scheme of the cool but exotic lobby was inspired by the terrazzo floor in the architects' own house

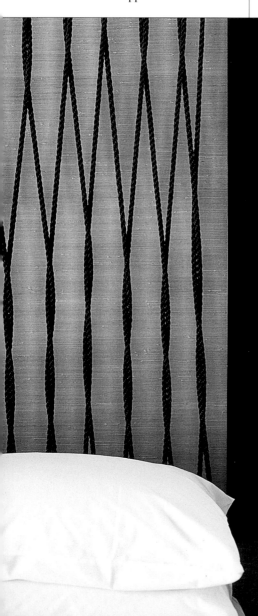

Twentieth-century designers both prominent and obscure are included in Wearstler's inspiring modernist cocktail

Kelly Wearstler objects to her interiors being described as "fifties" – her aim was to create something fresh and new

The modernist tile mural decorating the facade is a new creation by architects Henk Koning and Julie Eizenberg

Period designs by Warren Platner, Milo Baughman, Arne Jacobsen, Eero Saarinen, Alvar Aalto, Isamu Noguchi and George Nelson are confidently mixed with Thonet chairs, vintage finds and Wearstler's own designs. Lamps by George Nelson, tables by Noguchi and chairs by Aalto sit alongside her custom-designed bedheads in timber and black hemp, as well as her lounge chairs, lamps and ottomans. In the lobby, a Wearstler-designed copper-clad reception desk and a rosewood coffee table are combined with vintage 1950s furniture that she found in Paris, of all places. The rug that ties in the tones of green, blue and gray was commissioned from Angela Adams.

As in other hotels that Kelly Wearstler has designed, a consistent color scheme is very much part of the equation. For Avalon she decided on a palette of refreshingly cool blues and greens inspired by a blue terrazzo floor in Koning and Eizenberg's own home. For the walls, Wearstler commissioned Mark Edward Harris to shoot black and white semi-abstract images of the hotel's architecture. These were then simply framed and used to adorn the guestrooms. The larger suites also have oil paintings discovered in the fleamarkets of London and Paris. Down pillows and Frette linen round out the depth of attention to detail.

If you are the type that likes to cocoon in your room with a movie, Avalon's spacious rooms make it a good choice. But for those who want to go out, Avalon is in the heart of Beverly Hills, well placed for dinner at the Ivy, Matsuhisa, Maple Drive, Mako or Maestro; or for checking out the contemporary art scene at galleries such as Pace, Gagosian or Wildenstein; or for blowing your budget at the boutiques of Rodeo Drive. In short, all the attractions of LA's most glamorous district are within easy reach. Or you can enjoy the award-winning cuisine of the Avalon's Blue on Blue restaurant and never venture from your poolside cabana.

address Avalon Hotel, 9400 West Olympic Boulevard, Beverly Hills, California 90212

t +1 (310) 277 5221 **f** +1 (310) 277 4928 **e** info@korhotelgroup.com

room rates from $169

the standard, downtown

Bright red vibrating circular water beds in Star Trek-esque space pods, orange banquettes, white fifties plastic furniture, red Astroturf and a rooftop swimming pool (complete with nightly skinny dippers) – this isn't the kind of thing you expect to come across in the downtown business district of Los Angeles.

Until recently most actors would tell you they hate Downtown LA. They shoot a lot there, but only because they have to. After hours the district is dead, a ghost town of deserted office blocks. But the opening of the Standard, Downtown changed all that. A few years ago André Balazs, creator of New York's Mercer and LA's Chateau Marmont, invited me to come look over a new property he was considering. So, on a sunny winter's day, we stood together in the cavernous ground floor of an abandoned 1950s office building, the custom-built headquarters of an oil company. It was clear from the granite floors and bronze elevator doors that this had been a quality building, with some architectural integrity. But I admit, I was a little skeptical. To think of it as a hotel required a massive leap of imagination. Even revitalized and transformed, who would come here, and why? Downtown LA doesn't have the pull of Sunset Boulevard, or the

beaches of Santa Monica. Yet the day-to-day reality, as Balazs had observed, is that there is business to be done in LA. Law, accountancy and insurance firms and assorted multi-nationals all have offices in the handful of skyscrapers that make up Downtown LA. They regularly entertain business visitors – accommodation just around the corner might be not only practical, but in the hands of Balazs, also desirable.

As it turned out, the Standard, Downtown has not only captured this business niche, but more tellingly it's become a hit with the city's native nine-to-fivers. For the first time, LA suits have a place to go – for lunch in the yellow 1960s diner, for drinks in the pink and black lobby, for cocktails at the rooftop bar, and for clubbing by the pool after dark. Above all else, the Standard is a fun urban hangout with all the laid-back, warm-weather attitude of California. This is a city hotel in which the snowbound East Coast executive can enjoy some California lifestyle without compromising his or her work ethic. Just as importantly, like its sister hotel in Hollywood, the Standard, Downtown is also affordable – a good example to prove that design need not inflate a hotel's room rates. Better still, you wouldn't know it.

Thanks to the generosity of the original architecture, the rooms are tall and spacious with open-plan white mosaic-tiled bathrooms and the odd splash of sixties furniture. They are marketed like Gap T-shirts in small, medium, large and extra large, but even the small rooms are bigger than standard and all are equipped with state-of-the-art electronics.

If you have work to do in Downtown LA you can't go wrong with the Standard, but there are some insider's tips that could make your stay more enjoyable. If you opt for an extra-large room, for example (a massive loft-like space with a gigantic bathroom and monumental bath) do not – repeat, do not – be tempted to take the gargantuan black Roman foot that forms the sculptural centerpiece of your bathroom into the bath with you. The last guest to do this left it there while he partied upstairs, and returned to discover that urethane foam absorbs water like a sponge. The foot had soaked up the entire contents of the huge tub, leaving it weighing several tons. A cool grand was added to his bill: $800 to replace the sculpture, and $200 in labor to cut it into pieces so that it could be removed. Another tip: if you are shocked by nudity, don't be hanging around the pool after midnight. And be warned: the bright red capsules that stand like little spaceships beside the pool were designed for groups of up to twelve to enjoy cocktails sitting on the gently vibrating waterbeds. But usually you won't find more than two to a pod, and they aren't drinking cocktails.

The most unexpected effect of the Standard, Downtown has caught even its creators by surprise. Given the location they expected weekends to be quiet. But weekends at the Standard have started to be even more heavily booked than weekdays, and not by interstate business travelers but by suburban Angelinos seeking a taste of downtown high-rise life. Residents of LA's never-ending low-rise suburbs can be overheard gazing over the glass towers of Downtown LA saying things like "awesome dude – it's just like Chicago."

address The Standard, Downtown LA, 550 South Flower Street, Los Angeles, California 90071

t +1 (213) 892 8080 **f** +1 (213) 892 8686 **e** downtownla@standardhotel.com

room rates from $95

maison 140

The beauty of LA is that you are free to invent your own world. Or in the case of Brad Korzen and Kelly Wearstler, your own worlds.

Once upon a time the stars of Hollywood – old Hollywood – put all their personality into their houses. But that was back when stars did real interviews, the kind where they didn't have the questions weeks beforehand, or worse, delegated to personal publicists to feed the media pre-chewed content, as happens now. These days interiors and architecture in LA have gone down the same calculated road. What the stars wear, where they eat and where they live are no longer an expression of personality, they are the product of a meeting between image specialist, personal shopper, private dietician, publicist and PR company.

The result is that in the world of LA interiors, the only area of genuine innovation is in hotels. Why? Because something different makes an attractive proposition. And for the guest at least there is no risk. You spend a few nights living a fantasy – staying in an environment quite unlike your own, without making any commitment. You are not buying the room, after all, just renting it for the night. It's a liberating proposition, and one that Brad Korzen, property developer and hotelier, and

Kelly Wearstler, interior designer, have embraced enthusiastically. That's why their second hotel in Los Angeles bears little if any resemblance to the Avalon, their first.

Maison 140, a small, renovated brick townhouse, is a creation completely unto itself. The brochure describes it as "a mandarin french kiss in the heart of Beverly Hills" – purple prose indeed. Wearstler herself sums up her creation more pithily as "Pucci meets Louis XVI," while *Wallpaper* called it an "homage to David Hicks, where you can easily imagine Joan Collins having cocktails with Liberace." And for *W* magazine it is "a tiny lacquer red pastiche evoking the Paris of Colette."

It's true the interior spaces walk a fine line between courageous and camp, but as Korzen explains, the building – a brownstone walk-up built around 1939 – is so uncharacteristic for Beverly Hills that it was a natural opportunity to take a creative break from the mid-century modernism that is so prevalent in LA at the moment. They also opted to observe the trusty design dictum that when faced with smaller spaces it is better to go dark, busy and complex than bright and white. The entire reception, lounge and bar of Maison 140 comprise only 1,200 square feet, but this smallish scale is not

what you register when you enter. What you do notice are the deep Chinese red armchairs set rather plushly against black lacquered walls. You notice the David Hicks-style patterned red carpet and the antique mirrored panels detailed in the chinoiserie style. Admittedly it works better at night, but perhaps that's stating the obvious. My favorite guestrooms at Maison 140 continue the opium den theme from the lobby – lots of black, lots of red, chinoiserie-style wallpaper, and sage mandarins turned into bedside lamps. Different floors feature different color schemes, so if you are not into red and black, try the gray–ocher scheme featuring a yellow bamboo trellis wallpaper combined with furniture painted in tones of light gray.

This building used to be owned by Lillian Gish, a silent screen star who no doubt would have approved of the Shanghai Suzy boudoir renovation. But what kind of people choose Maison 140 today? My off-the-cuff answer would be Woody Allen-types – out-of-towners not particularly into LA's sun and surf lifestyle.

As an added plus, Maison 140 is extremely well located. In a town where it's virtually impossible to be without a car, you could just manage it staying here, provided you don't need to leave Beverly Hills. For shoppers there is no better location. Nestled between Santa Monica Boulevard and Wilshire Boulevard, the hotel is literally around the corner from the premier department stores and the boutiques of Rodeo Drive.

The 140 doesn't have its own pool, but it makes up for it by laying on pool privileges at the nearby Avalon Hotel. In any case, as any regular visitor would know, the sun-worship culture is changing fast, giving way to a sophistication that is more in keeping with LA's status as America's second largest city. Perhaps the most telling boast in the hotel's publicity kit is the fact that almost none of the contents of Maison 140 is available in any shop. This is the new criterion of the American elite: not being able to get it retail is a virtual guarantee of exclusivity.

address Maison 140, 140 South Lasky Drive, Beverly Hills, California 90212

t +1 (310) 281 4000 **f** +1 (310) 281 4001 **e** info@korhotelgroup.com

room rates from $149

viceroy

"What do you think of Kelly Wearstler's design?"an architect friend asked me. "I like it," was my response, "particularly the way a single color is the dominant design code for each new hotel. I like the fact that Maison 140 is red, the Avalon is aqua blue and that Estrella's signature is yellow." He laughed when I suggested the only shortcoming was that Wearstler hadn't yet done a green one. "You obviously haven't been to Viceroy," he replied.

Sure enough Santa Monica's Viceroy is Wearstler's design response in green. If one place was really waiting for a hotel like this, it was definitely Santa Monica. Art-wise, architecture-wise, design-wise, and restaurant-wise, this beachside suburb of Los Angeles has been getting more and more street-wise. Frank Gehry's 1991 headquarters for ad agency Chiat/Day is here, fronted by a pair of giant binoculars by Claes Oldenburg; celebrity chef Wolfgang Puck opened his Montana restaurant here; and Dennis Hopper moved his home and art collection here. Santa Monica is also possibly the first place in LA to introduce a traffic-free pedestrian zone. The only thing it didn't have was a hotel in step with its increasingly avant-garde personality. Admittedly there is a beachfront hotel,

Shutters, a mix between four-star hotel and beachside cabana that has long been a favorite with LA visitors who prefer to be by the ocean. However, few would argue that its beige-on-beige style has now dated a bit.

So the opening of Viceroy in July 2002 was perfectly timed. This was the first new hotel to open in Santa Monica in three years, the result of a complete refurbishment of a boxy, office-like 1969 hotel building located on the corner of Pico Boulevard and Ocean Avenue, just a block away from the sea. It only took a few months for Viceroy to become the hangout of choice in Santa Monica, and with a broader demographic than you might imagine. The design scheme, courtesy of kwid (Kelly Wearstler Interior Design), manages to appeal to the older set that used to have tea at Shutters as well as the cutting-edge art world and the actors and directors who choose to live near the beach. According to Wearstler, the inspiration for the color scheme came from the huts and shacks at Myrtle Beach, South Carolina, where she spent summer vacations as a child. The floors are that pickled, faded gray of weathered timber and the green of the kind one associates with old fishing boats. Whatever the inspiration, the colors work.

W magazine called the style a mixture of Regency and driftwood. Wearstler herself describes it as "modern colonial" – one of those catch phrases, like shabby chic, that only Californians can get away with. In this case the colonial theme is expressed in the wing chairs upholstered in bottle green wool complete with white embroidered monograms that are arranged in conversation groupings throughout the lobby. Then there are the Royal Worcester plates hung on the walls inside and out. The modern side of the design equation is supplied by black-and-white deep-buttoned sofas, glass coffee tables, white leather footstools and metallic silver lampshades.

The objective was to create something fresh, and in that respect Viceroy has succeeded. But at the same time, the ambience, particularly around the pools and in the gardens surrounding the restaurant, is of a poolside cabana from another age. In fact it's an atmosphere straight out of the movies. Among the poolside palms, guests can recline in Moroccan-inspired cabanas elegantly appointed in shades of gray with green accents, or, for those who prefer to be out in the open, tall chairs upholstered in white vinyl sit under swaying palms. Most effective of all are the two perfectly symmetrical, and identical, pools…so much more chic than just one. Apparently, the dual pool came about by accident – often the case with design innovations. It was to have been just one, but in the middle of the excavation the builders came across a water main beneath the very center of the proposed pool site. Also spilling outdoors, where even more plates adorn the gun-metal gray walls, is the Whist Restaurant. Since opening this has become one of the most sought-after reservations in Santa Monica.

So there you have it – glamour, innovation, style – this green hotel is all you could want in Los Angeles…unless, that is, your penchant is for pink, in which case you'll just have to wait for Korzen and Wearstler's next hotel.

---

address Viceroy, 1819 Ocean Avenue, Santa Monica, California 90401

t +1 (310) 260 7500   **f** +1 (310) 260 7518   **e** info@viceroysantamonica.com

room rates from $249

the beach house

One day most American inns will look like this – no chintz, no four-posters, no marine knickknacks, in fact no knickknacks at all. It's not that I have anything against four-posters, sleigh beds or highboys; in fact I really appreciate American Federal period antiques. But the fact is that these days to furnish a hotel with the real thing, or even passable imitations, would be unfeasibly expensive. So what you actually get in most cozy, period-style bed and breakfasts are copies of copies, usually third rate. The more Federal pieces are imitated, the more expensive and unattainable the genuine article becomes. And thus authenticity and historic merit keep slipping further and further out of reach. It's a depressing trend that has nowhere to go but down.

Thank goodness one hotel entrepreneur had the good sense to ditch the whole package. The Beach House is, decoratively speaking, a big breath of fresh air. Built in 1891, this is one of Kennebunkport's original bed and breakfasts, but its recent renovation has taken it right into the twenty-first century. Guestrooms are furnished in a palette of sand and slate with dark brown accents – the neutral tones of the spectacular coastal setting. On the walls there are black and white photographic prints of

local New England beaches and the furniture consists of simply upholstered pieces and lots of rattan, executed in darkly stained shades. There are some wrought-iron Victorian beds, but no quilts and no tea containers turned into lamps. Style-wise, the Beach House pours cold water on the notion that clutter equals cozy. This place has a coziness derived not from masses of stuff but from the inviting warmth of ambient light and natural textures such as rattan, linen, wool and wood. On the ground floor there's a roaring fire to take the nip out of the evening air, and deep couches in which to slouch with a book. And there's the typical Victorian wraparound porch, which in this case offers an amazing view of the Maine coastline.

Maine's southern coast is quieter, and some say prettier, than the better known Booth Bay or Bar Harbor, to which tourists flock to see real lobstermen at work. The beaches are sand rather than pebble, and the water, naturally, is of a slightly more accommodating temperature. OK, it's not the Bahamas, but as they say around here "it's the Atlantic, it's an ocean, it's cold – it's good for you."

It's called Beach House, so what about the beaches? Gooch's Beach is a local stretch of sand whose backdrop of Victorian mansions is reminiscent of Newport, though less ostentatiously grand. Nearby York Beach is the favorite, particularly its Long Sands and Short Sands – one a mile-long broad expanse of sand, the other a sheltered cove. If you fancy a dune to yourself then you should venture to Ogunquit Beach, a stretch of Cape Cod-like dunes that extend for three or four miles. Further north the same stretch of sandy hills changes its name to Footbridge Beach and then Moody Beach, a surfers' favorite.

But this being Maine, one of the most unspoiled states in the Union, there's more to do than simply go to the beach. Whale-watching is one of the many options. For $30 a day, you can take the twenty-mile boat trip out to Jeffrey's Ledge, where humpbacks, finbacks and minke whales congregate to feed. Even massive blue whales have occasionally been spotted here. Or you could charter the "Ugly Anne," a no-nonsense fishing boat straight out of *Perfect Storm* for some real deep sea fishing. This is not angling for marlin, however, but the slightly

more sedate sport of trawling for cod, haddock and sea bass – which, by the way, you are expected to eat if you catch them. If your tastes are more luxurious, you could also go lobstering for a day. Outside Perkins Cove you can watch Maine's lobstermen bait and set traps and haul out the feisty crustaceans with apparent ease. Or you can try it yourself, though no one will guarantee you won't lose a finger.

When I got here in early October, it was already too chilly to contemplate a dip or even going out on a fishing boat without more serious clothing than I had in my suitcase. But this is a place where the changing seasons are a visual drama, and there was plenty to compensate. The leaves were changing color in spectacular fashion, and sunrise was well worth getting out of bed for. The beaches were deserted apart from the odd local out walking a dog, and the clam shacks in town were doing a roaring trade. For anyone seeking the fresh-faced America of more innocent times, Kennebunkport and the Beach House fit the bill perfectly.

---

address The Beach House, PO Box 560C, 211 Beach Avenue, Kennebunkport, Maine 04046

t +1 (207) 967 3850 **f** +1 (207) 967 4719 **e** innkeeper@beachhseinn.com

room rates from $255

the white barn inn

Bumped by Bush – I should have had a sticker made. The story starts in New York City. I was booked to appear live on CNN to answer questions about my ten favorite hotels in as many soundbites as I could conjure in the space of seven or so minutes. There I was in an all-black room, wired up, staring at a screen, with a mike in my ear so I could be given a countdown to live on air. "Just a few minutes more," the voice kept repeating…after an an hour and a half of "just a few minutes more" the voice finally said: "I'm so very sorry. We've run out of time. Perhaps we can reschedule." Apparently George W. Bush had decided to call an impromptu press conference that morning, and all of CNN's programming was adjusted accordingly. In TV talk, I'd been bumped by Bush.

Less than a month later I was back. Same studio, same black room, same mike in my ear, same countdown…almost the same stumbling block. Because believe it or not, Bush decided to hold another impromptu press conference. Fortunately this time, thanks to some fast footwork in Atlanta, they got me on air ahead of him. The joke in the corridors of CNN New York that day was "Hey, there's the guy who almost got bumped by Bush again."

They had no idea. The following week I was trying to organize the Maine leg of my cross-country adventure when the staff from the White Barn Inn came back very apologetically: "I'm so very sorry. Normally it would not be a problem, but we cannot accommodate you or anyone else for that matter because we've been completely booked out by…George Bush." You only need the faintest passing interest in American politics to know that Kennebunkport is *the* summer address of the Bush family – winter in Houston, summer in Kennebunkport, Maine. This time, George Bush, Jr., was visiting his parents and the White Barn Inn was fully occupied by his entourage. I'd been bumped by Bush – *again*.

In fact the Bush connection to the White Barn Inn was no great surprise. This established American inn is bang in the middle of Wasp country. I doubt there's a place anywhere in the United States with more Stars and Stripes to the acre. Every porch, every house, every shop, every restaurant, church, town hall, and even all the New England clam shacks – if they haven't got the flag flying, they have it plastered against the wall. With its signature clapboard houses and lobsterboat charm, this part of New England is the clean-faced, bright-eyed

embodiment of all-American life – inspiration for fashion labels like Tommy Hilfiger and Ralph Lauren, and a particularly appropriate place for a former Republican president to have a summer house.

Despite doubtless having at least one talented chef in residence, George Bush, Sr., is a regular dinner guest at the White Barn Inn. In accolades and awards from the gourmet, wine and travel press, the inn has swept the board as the best country restaurant in New England. In fact for many travelers, the restaurant, not Kennebunkport, is the destination. It has the kind of following that Les Trois Gros or Michel Bras have in France. Set in a pair of old 1860s barns, the dining room is a towering space of rugged weathered beams and joists. The furnishings, in contrast, are more in the manner of a formal European restaurant complete with an army of formally dressed and trained, mainly European waiters. It's both cozy and elegant, yet there's no mistaking you are in New England. (Just in case you should forget, there's a huge American flag hanging down from the rafters.) Where the barn's old sliding doors would have been there is now a gigantic *Alice in Wonderland* still life of immense pumpkins.

In terms of accommodation, the inn's colonial building is furnished in traditional Federal style – lots of red and gold, antiques and polished dark wooden floors. It also delivers modern comforts like big bathrooms, power showers, huge televisions, DVDs, and internet connections without impinging on the historic character and charm. It came as no surprise to discover that the White Barn Inn is owned by an Aussie, Laurence Bongiorno, who used to be a manager of Melbourne's Hyatt Regency. This explains the thoroughly professional yet unpretentious presentation. It's the kind of retreat where you can enjoy long late breakfasts, big lunches, afternoon tea, the odd walk on the nearby beach, dozing off by the fireplace and a long delicious dinner at night. But be warned: I can't guarantee you won't bump into a Bush.

address The White Barn Inn, PO Box 560C, 37 Beach Avenue, Kennebunkport, Maine 04046

t +1 (207) 967 2321 **f** +1 (207) 967 1100 **e** innkeeper@whitebarninn.com

room rates from $305

the porches inn

Porches is an enigma. Why, you might ask, would anyone want to come to an old industrial mill town in a remote pocket of the Massachusetts Berkshires?

The answer, in case you hadn't heard, is MASS MoCA. The story of MASS MoCA is already a legend – a fairy tale starring a down-and-out mill town in a picturesque back corner of the Berkshire hills. A century ago North Adams was home to the Arnold Print & Dye Works, a huge textile mill that employed three-quarters of the local population. When the mill foundered, it was taken over by a company producing electrical components. When that too foundered in the mid-1980s, so did the town. With the closure of the factory, North Adams went into economic freefall and its twelve-acre Victorian industrial complex became a derelict eyesore. North Adams was the fairy-tale frog and the mill was its wart.

In these post-industrial times, we are familiar with the idea of industrial structures being renovated and reincarnated for entirely new purposes. But a complex in excess of twelve acres that is a four-hour drive from New York and three from Boston? Now that does test the imagination. Yet today the Massachusetts Museum of Contemporary Art is a major player on the world art scene. It is not a museum in the MoMA or Getty mold: it doesn't have the collections, nor the curated polish. Instead it is a venue oriented predominantly towards performance and installation art. It certainly has the space to allow these artists full scope of expression. It is already the largest contemporary art museum in the United States, and when further planned development is complete it will be the largest museum in the United States, period.

Create an extraordinary art venue, make it an unprecedented success, and pretty soon you can expect to need a hotel to accommodate visitors who make the trek from New York, Boston and further afield. But in fact the Porches Inn, adjacent to the MASS MoCA complex, was less the child of logic than a case of "what on earth do we do with that eyesore?" The view from the museum was of a hopelessly derelict row of timber workers' cottages on the wrong side of the track. Think *Flashdance* and you get a feel for the aesthetic. Still, anyone with the vision to create a museum on this scale couldn't fail to see potential in a row of abandoned shacks, and the creative driving forces behind MASS MoCA were convinced someone would be prepared to take it on.

The color schemes of Porches' guestrooms are original and seductive, ranging from earth reds to lilac grays

Bathrooms are simple and white. The mirror frames were made from timber salvaged from the original cottages

Across the street, occupying the former mill works, is the largest museum in the United States

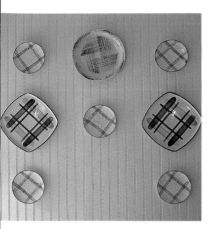

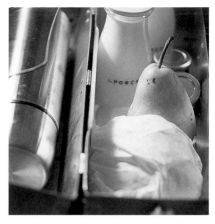

Porches was created from a row of
derelict workers' cottages whose cozy
kitsch decor inspired its interior style

All the guestrooms have different color
schemes and are paneled in simple timber
tongue-and-groove wainscoting

In tribute to the town's blue-collar roots,
breakfast comes in a worker's lunchbox
complete with a thermos of coffee

Enter Nancy Fitzpatrick, part of a family who know a bit about running hotels here amid the hills, forests and lakes of the Berkshires. The Fitzpatricks are proprietors of the Red Lion Inn, a two hundred year old New England establishment that has a considerable reputation for its restaurant. Porches is Nancy's contemporary yang to the Red Lion's more traditional yin.

In construction terms what she undertook was less a renovation than a total rebuild. Every one of the timber houses was gutted and deconstructed. When they were put back together again, something interesting happened: on the one hand they remained what they were – typical mill workers' homes; but they were also transformed into funky accommodation the likes of which the Massachusetts countryside has never known. Bathrooms are big, white and contemporary, with clean lines, huge showers, and custom-made toiletries; rooms have DVD players, state-of-the-art internet connections, well-stocked mini bars and entertainment set-ups more typical of big city hotels. But the interiors have a kitsch flavor that is at once appropriate, authentic and fun. Hanging on the tongue-and-groove paneled walls are paint-by-numbers canvases and plates – the type of faintly embarrassing plates that you find in tourist souvenir shops, with lurid drawings and cheesy inscriptions like "Florida, Sunshine State" or "Iowa, Corn Capital of the USA." These proletarian design touches – what the people at Porches describe as "industrial granny chic" – are inspired. They pay ironic but affectionate homage to the generations of factory workers who lived in these houses. It's a clever ploy that makes the rocking chairs in the guestrooms and the pumpkins on the veranda seem somehow contemporary, like part of a modern figurative painting. And it pervades every aspect of the Porches experience, including the room service breakfast – juice, croissant and coffee arrive in a rectangular dome-topped aluminium container with a handle…a worker's lunchbox, to be exact.

address The Porches Inn, 231 River Street, North Adams, Massachusetts 01247
t +1 (413) 664 0400 **f** +1 (413) 664 0401 **e** info@porches.com
room rates from $125

wheatleigh

This could well be the best hotel in the United States. The building is a magnificent Italianate mansion, the location is the picturesque Berkshires, one of the prettiest parts of New England, the town is Lenox – famous for its gentility, its classical music scene and its former resident Edith Wharton. The interiors are the most immaculate example of New York-based design and architecture duo Tsao McKown's work, the food is easily the best in Massachusetts, if not New England, and the service beats that of any city hotel I know. Wheatleigh has cottoned on to the kind of personal attention to detail that made the Aman chain so successful. There's no ugly front desk, no bureaucracy to greet you when you arrive via the immaculately groomed gravel driveway. Valets whisk away your car, your suitcases are transferred to your room and registration is a mere matter of signing your name. At night, while you are being spoiled by chef J. Bryce Whittlesey, someone sneaks into your room to turn down your bed and lower the lights. People with an Aman habit will be used to this treatment, but here in the upper northwest corner of New England it's an eye-opener.

The property was originally commissioned in 1893 by Henry H. Cook – New York

financier-banker, director of railroads and real estate tycoon – as a wedding present for his daughter Georgie, who was bringing a title into the family by her marriage to Carlos de Heredia, a real-life Spanish count. Even by the lavish standards of the area, Cook did his level best to raise the bar in terms of extravagance. He invited Boston architects Peabody and Stearns to design the house based on a sixteenth-century Florentine palazzo, and imported raw materials and 150 craftsmen from Italy to finish the exteriors and interiors to authentic perfection. Tiffany was brought in to design and manufacture an impressive pair of leaded stained-glass windows, and, lest the garden suffer by comparison, no less than Frederick Law Olmsted, designer of New York's Central Park, was employed to create an outdoor space worthy of the grand mansion. When their "country cottage" was finished the Count and Countess used it for about six weeks a year. The rest of the time they resided on Fifth Avenue in New York.

When Lin and Susan Simon first encountered Wheatleigh, it was being run as a hotel – rather badly. Even so, its pedigree was impossible to ignore. Susan Simon, an art gallery owner from Chicago, and Lin,

a successful lawyer, made a decision on the spot. "We knew this was an irreplaceable property, and once places like this are allowed to go to ruin you lose them forever." Their impromptu act of real estate largesse left them with a hotel that they ran for the next fifteen years, all the while making improvements and renovations, but always in the existing style.

Then came the turning point. The chandelier, a dazzling nineteenth-century creation in crystal, shattered into a million pieces. Other people would be devastated. For the Simons it was their day of liberation, a wake-up call giving them the push they needed to transform Wheatleigh into a contemporary interpretation of classic taste and style. It was time, in their words, "to reinvent Wheatleigh for the present."

Four years later Wheatleigh re-emerged as something unique: a grand American country estate redefined in an inspiring contemporary manner. The courage to take this step was all the Simons' – the new Wheatleigh is definitely their baby. But the finesse in which it was executed is to the considerable credit of Calvin Tsao and Zack McKown. Their sophisticated international eclecticism is like a powerful potion – a design opiate. The reinvention of Wheatleigh was founded on rigorous research. Before touching a single brick or plank, Tsao and McKown studied old photographs and read up all the existing history. Their goal was to preserve the property's romance while updating its style. Brushed velvet in silvery tones, silk cushions in shades of copper, bronze and gold, one-off pieces found in China, Morocco, Antwerp, Paris and London, their own pared-down furniture designs: the resulting ensemble is sensuous, romantic, graceful and understated in a way that is almost impossible to convey in words. It's the kind of place you might expect a world-class pianist to live – which is eerily close to the truth given that the late Leonard Bernstein's favorite room used to be the Treehouse suite.

address Wheatleigh, Hawthorne Road, Lenox, Massachusetts 01240

t +1 (413) 637 0610 **f** +1 (413) 637 4507 **e** info@wheatleigh.com

room rates from $425

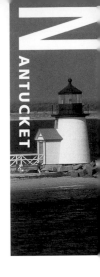

v n h

Nantucket is a pretty place: historic, unspoiled, full of character, understated, friendly…almost perfect. It might even *be* perfect if only for the fact that its signature style treads a very fine line between classy and clichéd. There's so much gingham, distressed timber, basketweave, embroidered quilts and old ship curios in Nantucket that the island comes dangerously close to being a theme park of its own aesthetic. Every house is shingle-sided or clapboard-paneled, every window is a sash window, every door has raised and fielded panels, every other house has fanlights above the entrance, and they are all stained or weathered to a palette of heritage shades. Then there are the shops – there are more antique shops here than on London's Pimlico Road, all selling yet more quilts and gingham. Shops, bars and restaurants all have names like the Quaker House, the Plymouth Inn, the Even Keel, the Captain's Table, the Bosun's Locker, the Skipper's this, the Sailor's that – for the slightly skeptical urbanite, it can all get way too cute.

All of this is why the Vanessa Noel Hotel is such a clever move. Outside, it's like the rest of the town – sash-windowed and shingle-sided, gray and white, all as it should be. Inside is a different story: no wallpaper, no gingham, no nautical mementoes, no tea canisters turned into table lamps, no quilts. There's not a New England cliché in sight. Guest rooms have not a thing on the walls: nothing, *nada, niente*. They are distinguished by no more than a cream and white color scheme, very beautiful old floorboards, some refined pieces of wicker furniture and luxurious linens. Yet since opening in summer 2002 these sparse spaces have been a huge success. That may come as a surprise to some, but in a town that is a visual cacophony of decorative detail, the serenity of VNH is truly a haven. It isn't just that these rooms are reassuringly anti-kitsch, they are also very much in keeping with the true attraction of Nantucket – the dunes, the beaches, and the ocean. Fresh air and nature are this island's real drawing cards, not shopping.

That said, the shop that stops the most pedestrian traffic on one of Nantucket's main streets is the Vanessa Noel shoe boutique. Noel is a young, New York-based shoe designer who has been touted as the next Jimmy Choo. She has long spent every summer in Nantucket and opened her boutique here back in 1994. With VNH she has followed in the footsteps of Donatella Versace, the Ferragamo family, and Bulgari in expanding from the fashion business

V N H
VANESSA NOEL HOTEL

into hotels. When you think about it, this makes perfect sense: these are in essence just different ways of marketing lifestyle. And it certainly helps in getting a new hotel talked about: a proprietor with a recognized name and style means the press are almost guaranteed to sit up and take notice.

Fortunately, unlike the Versace hotels, which are even more gaudy than the clothes, Vanessa Noel's first venture shows real restraint. Yet it's not without the twist that has become her signature. The lobby for instance is a clean, sparse affair, with handsome dark wooden floors…decorated with nothing more than a bowl of goldfish. The brick fireplace has the obligatory US flag above it…except that on closer inspection the flag turns out to have shoes instead of stars; ditto for the stripes. On one side of the lobby is the entrance to the Vanno bar, the island's only caviar bar, which also doubles as a restaurant. Its wooden banquettes are upholstered in faux leopardskin, there are two indoor swings suspended from

the ceiling, and the walls are covered in plastic privet hedges, a neat reference to the perfect lawns to be found everywhere in Nantucket. On the other side of the lobby there's a Vanessa Noel shoe boutique with Starck leopardskin carpeting.

I suspect that the only people who are not entirely impressed with VNH are husbands hoping for an early getaway to the beach – not much chance with a woman's shoe shop directly in the way. Oh, and the taxi drivers. Fresh off the ferry from the mainland (two and a half hours from Hyannis Port), I couldn't find a single taxi driver who had ever heard of the Vanessa Noel Hotel. One driver even got quite indignant, insisting that as she had been born here and had lived all her life on tiny Nantucket, the hotel I was looking for must be on Martha's Vineyard. On reflection, it was my mistake. I should have asked for the shoe shop – although I suspect they would have been even more confused. "What, you plan to stay at a shoe shop?"

---

address VNH, #5 Chestnut Street, Nantucket, Massachusetts 02554

t +1 (508) 228 5300 f +1 (508) 228 8995

room rates from $340

the shaker inn

According to the manager of the Shaker Inn, his European visitors know more about the Shakers than the Americans. But then don't we all take less notice of what's in our own backyard? So who are – or rather, were – the Shakers? Like the Amish, the Mennonites and the Mormons, the Shakers were a separatist religious sect with some seriously strict beliefs – celibacy, hard labor, the confession of sin. The name comes from their strange trance-like worship that fascinated outsiders. They would shriek and sing, tremble and shake. They were the Moonies of their day. Male and female Shakers lived together but separately in boarding-school-like dormitories called Great Houses, men at one end, women at the other. Each sex had its own staircase, and although they ate in the same dining room – men on one side, women on the other – meals were held in total silence.

But not all their time was spent in prayer. Shakers were taught to "put your hands to work and your heart to God." The women kept busy in the communal kitchens, or with sewing, embroidery, knitting or weaving, while the men spent many an hour honing their skills in the carpentry workshops. They made nothing fancy, mind you – needless decoration was almost as immoral as sex. Their disciplined

approach to life and art resulted in an oeuvre of craft distinguished by simple but beautifully made furniture. Stair banisters, for example, perfectly shaped and elegantly curved, would be cut from carefully matched black cherry. Mies van der Rohe may have coined the phrase "God is in the detail," but the Shakers beat him to it in practice by a century. The movement left behind an impressive collection of stuff: barns, workshops, meeting rooms, churches and Great Houses. But as a movement it had a fatal flaw: renouncing sex meant there were no little Shakers to pick up the minimalist baton. Once upon a time they numbered in the tens of thousands in communities all over New England, and as far away as Kentucky. Today, there are only a handful of devotees left in a depleted community in Maine.

My first real-life encounter with the Shaker heritage was the Hancock Shaker village in Massachusetts. Beautifully preserved, this was an eye-opener not just to the skill of Shaker craftsmanship but to its inventiveness. The famous round Shaker barn, for instance, was an ingenious labor-saving method of keeping animals fed throughout the winter. In the fall, hay was piled high in the middle while cows stood on ramps around the perimeter.

Symmetry and simplicity were the values most prized in Shaker craft, and they still distinguish the Shaker Inn

Shaker communities were completely self-sufficient. This red barn sheltered the cattle they raised

Thankfully, the Shaker Inn's restaurant does not maintain the Shaker tradition of dining in total silence

The red barns and verdant countryside go perfectly with the inn's simple white walls and blue and green woodwork

The checkered bedspreads, sourced in Shaker archives, were discovered in a Martha Stewart range at Kmart!

The bell tower atop the six-story dwelling would once have called the brethren to meals

Ensuite bathrooms were created in spaces that used to function as dressing rooms

Set among the hills of New Hampshire, Enfield Shaker Village is the epitome of the American Country bucolic ideal

Orderly living was paramount for the Shakers. Chairs not in use were hung on pegs on the walls

The Shaker dwelling at Enfield was one of very few to be constructed from stone. It is also one of the largest

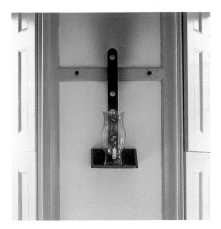

"Tis a gift to be simple" – the Shaker creed shaped every detail of their lives, including their system of moveable lamps

The hotel's furniture, like this rocking chair, faithfully reproduces original Shaker designs

The Shaker Inn's proportions, light and architectural details recall the seductive qualities of early Georgian architecture

The historic details and color scheme have been respected throughout the interior of the Shaker Inn

With their original dimensions intact, the guestrooms are wonderfully sunny and spacious

The Shakers built separate houses for their most senior brethren, although everyone came together at mealtimes

The Shaker Inn is so relaxed and peaceful that many guests do not even bother to close their doors

Storage, storage and more storage – the Shakers' solemn commitment to an orderly life is a bonus for modern guests

As winter progressed and the pile diminished, the cows gradually made their way around the ramp, eating their way down in a kind of agrarian version of the Guggenheim, New York. The only problem at Hancock was that in the effort to keep things spick and span, the managers were as strict if not stricter than the Shakers themselves. The place was exclusively staffed by people of traffic-cop mentality.

The Shaker Inn in Enfield, New Hampshire, is completely different. As little as possible has been altered since the Shakers were in residence so as a hotel experience it's eccentric yet surprisingly comfortable. Rooms are huge and filled with light, the floors are laid with big broad planks and all the cupboards are classic Shaker built-ins. Private bathrooms have been installed in what were closets between rooms, and most of the furniture follows original Shaker designs. Breakfast, lunch and dinner are served in the dining room of the stone Great House; the food, appropriately, is basic but delicious. There are still two staircases with original black

cherry banisters, but these days men and women are free to use either. One of the elders' meeting rooms has been converted to a bar, and another smaller room can be booked as a private dining space. Perhaps unexpectedly there's an open, warm, friendly camaraderie that pervades the place. The meeting room on the first floor is used for craft workshops; while I was staying, there was a quilt convention under way. More unexpected still, the hotel has become a hangout for New Hampshire locals. They regularly drop in for dinner, or for an impromptu game of backgammon in the bar.

Which begs the question: what would the Shakers have thought of all these people not only enjoying themselves, not only sleeping together but – God forbid – using each others' staircases? My bet is that they would be astounded by the longevity of their simple handcraft, and the respect in which it is held. They might even kick themselves for not having the foresight to make some little Shakers to keep their traditions alive.

address The Shaker Inn, 24 Caleb Dyer Lane, Enfield, New Hampshire 03748

t +1 (603) 632 4900 **f** +1 (603) 632 4554

room rates from $105

international house

Voodoo, jazz, Cajun cooking, Creole dialect, zydeco music… New Orleans has to rank as the most exotic city destination in the United States. Two centuries have now passed since the French government sold the vast tract of land known as the Louisiana Purchase to the fledgling republic of the United States, but the influence of France is still boldly evident here. The language is peppered with French phrases – streets are called *rue*, and you hear *le* and *la* used in front of English as well as French words. Dining is far more formal than anywhere else in the United States. In fact the only thing Louisianians love more than food is music – not the banal top twenty radio tunes that are exactly the same anywhere in the world but their own innovative and soulful bluegrass, jazz and zydeco.

International House was created to express both the uniqueness of New Orleans and its status as an international city. Yet at first glance, the hotel doesn't look or feel very New Orleans at all. If anything, from the outside it might just as well be a hotel in New York. This is because the local references are deliberately subtle and low-key, intended to reveal themselves slowly. The exterior architecture of this former international trade center would appear to be an example of pure classicism, with a rusticated granite base and ornate upper capitals; but upon investigation, you discover that details such as the handmade glass lanterns that grace the entrance were designed and made by Drew Bevolo, a third-generation New Orleans lantern maker whose family business still operates in the French Quarter. Inside the 23-foot-high lobby the same subtle tribute to local culture continues. The reception desk adorned with a back-lit grid of woven forged iron is not just an attractive decorative detail, but a reference to the delicate wrought-iron work that was originally introduced to New Orleans by the Spanish, another culture that has left its stamp on this city. The three chandeliers that hang in the lofty lobby were created by a Louisiana native, Guy Martin, using a mix of materials and decorative detail that are again evocative of local signatures.

The design of International House is analogous to a German car: the more you investigate the way it's put together, the more you are impressed by its quality. If all you are looking for is luxuriously comfortable accommodation in a central location near the French Quarter, International House is perfect.

International House has one of the best collections of black-and-white jazz photography in the country

In the Loa Bar, Haitian voodoo themes are blended with those of Catholicism to produce a seductive cultural hybrid

The soaring spaces of the lobby are softened by the sculptural wrought-iron latticework adorning the reception desk

The Loa Bar is a popular place to hang out after a visit to the French Quarter, which is literally next door

This impressively grand building, with its classically detailed facade, was originally an international trade center

The interiors are cool, calm and contemporary, with the odd flash of color introduced by modern artworks

But if you want more than that – if you want to stay in a place that reflects the fact that you are in New Orleans, then you will be impressed by the way local elements have been so intricately woven into the very fiber of this hotel.

The candle-lit Loa Bar just off the lobby is a particularly popular destination. Had I not been told that *loa* are voodoo divine spirits, I might never have picked up on the voodoo references. In New Orleans the local Catholic religion is heavily laced with voodoo tradition from Haiti, and this spiritual mix was the design inspiration behind Loa's ecclesiastical touches such as the church window mirrors that decorate the spaces of the lower bar. Exclusively lit by flickering candlelight, Loa is more than just a drinking hole, it's a nightly New Orleans ritual.

The city setting is the continual sub-theme of the interior spaces. Guestrooms showcase the hotel's substantial collection of black-and-white jazz photography, both vintage and contemporary. This includes pictures of local stars by legendary photographer Herman Leonard, whose images of Louis Armstrong, Billie Holiday, Dizzy Gillespie and Duke Ellington helped define the Jazz Age.

International House's contemporary style with a dash of New Orleans flavor was the brainchild of local real estate developer Sean Cummings. But Cummings doesn't look or sound like any real estate developer I have met before. He likes to quote Frank Lloyd Wright and the architectural theories of Aldo Rossi, which deal not only with the notion of cultural appropriateness but also with the building as urban artifact, a concept that goes deeper than shapes and measurements. Cummings is interested in the way that people respond to buildings, and the way that buildings can embody authenticity and life. He loves cities, because here in particular these intangibles connect us to generations present, past and future. An idealist he may be – the John Lennon of hotel development – but I believe he's on the right track.

---

address International House, 221 Camp Street, New Orleans, Louisiana 70130

t +1 (504) 553 9550 **f** +1 (504) 553 9560 **e** resagent@ihhotel.com

room rates from $189

loft 523

"Our perception of space has incredible effects on us. Ultimately it is about our identity: who we are and why we are. Not a mere matter." The words are David Hockney's, but the confidence to quote them in a hotel brochure belongs to the people behind Loft 523.

Even to call a hotel a loft these days is a bold move, given how overused the word has become. It used to have a more specific meaning. A loft was a former industrial or commercial building – some kind of factory or warehouse – that had been converted into a living space. The key characteristic of this kind of interior was unencumbered space, without internal partitions beyond the odd structural pillar. For a while, the loft space was the urban architectural equivalent of the great outdoors. That is, until the property developers jumped aboard. All of a sudden, every other new apartment on sale was a loft. Then came the term "loft style," meaning little more than an apartment with white walls and contemporary kitchen and bathroom.

So I was understandably hesitant when I heard about a new hotel in New Orleans calling itself a loft. I've heard it all before. Happily, my reservations were unfounded. Loft 523, along with the Mercer in New York, is one of very few

real loft spaces to have been successfully reinterpreted as hotels. Most importantly, Loft 523 has the right bones. The five-story building dating to 1880 is a former carriage and dry-goods warehouse located at 523 Gravier Street in the Central Business District of New Orleans, an area that saw quite some innovation in architectural design in that period. To withstand the wear and tear of constant loading and unloading, this warehouse was built to last, and hence its heavy timber beams, cast iron columns, wide plank flooring, and masonry archways survive to this day.

If unencumbered space is the hallmark of a loft, 523 certainly measures up. The eighteen guestrooms average 600 square feet, and the bathrooms another 120. They are easily the size of a small apartment in London, New York or Paris – except that there is nothing about these spaces that feels like a conventional apartment. Much to the credit of Sean Cummings and his team – New Orleans architect Brooks Graham and designer John Chrestia – the fiber of the original building was left not only intact but exposed. Sprinkler pipes, rough timber beams, blistered brick walls, slightly crooked cast iron columns: all the textures and telltale features of the building's

utilitarian past are preserved and incorporated into the decoration. In places the original crumbling plaster was left on the walls and the elevator – not original – has been clad with sections of the old pressed-tin ceiling.

It takes style and confidence to know when to renew and when to leave well enough alone, and that's the balance they got very right at Loft 523. Together with the rugged architectural setting, guests are treated to such uncommon design luxuries as egg-shaped limestone "Spoon" baths by Agape, Finnish Vola taps, Frette linen and Herman Miller desk chairs, as well as wireless internet access, state-of-the-art sound systems and enormous television screens. Some of the larger rooms go one step further, featuring very sculptural and beautiful studio lamps by Mariano Fortuny, the great Spanish-born artist, couturier and designer who worked in Venice at the turn of the last century.

With hammered copper doors, twelve-foot-high ceilings, floor-to-ceiling windows letting in masses of natural light, polished concrete floors, rugged industrial textures, and a wealth of original design details, Loft 523 stands out as a highly individual place. But ironically, I doubt most of the drinkers in the downstairs bar have even noticed those beautifully imperfect nineteenth-century cast iron columns. What they come for is the ambience and the music. This is New Orleans, after all. There is regular live blues and bluegrass in the bar. If you were to start waxing poetic about the huge slabs of limestone on the bathroom floor, I'm sure their eyes would quickly glaze over.

But that's just one more plus of Loft 523 – it couldn't be precious if it wanted to be. It's a fun place that design-wise happens to be miles ahead of the game. With a multicultural room service menu, two penthouse lofts with their own 1,000-square-foot Zen terrace gardens, and a location just a stone's throw from New Orleans' famous French Quarter, I can only foresee one long-term problem with Loft 523 – you won't be able to get in. It's the kind of problem any hotel is happy to have.

address Loft 523, 523 Gravier Street, New Orleans, Louisiana 70130
t +1 (504) 200 6523   f +1 (504) 200 6522   e resagent@loft523.com
room rates from $199

city club hotel

Twenty years ago you would only stay in Midtown if you happened to be a member of the Harvard Club, or if your sensibilities allowed you to overlook the slightly shabby state of the Algonquin, one-time haunt of Dorothy Parker and her literary pals. Midtown was for the rag trade. All Manhattan's best hotels were further uptown or downtown; areas such as SoHo, the Village and Tribeca had the odd bed and breakfast, nothing more.

Then came the phenomenon of Morgans. Ex-Studio 54 impresarios Ian Schrager and Steve Rubell spotted the appeal of individual, architecturally sophisticated, European-style hotels, and invited French designer Andrée Putman to create this small hotel on Madison. Its startling success was followed by the opening of the Philippe Starck-designed Paramount, a budget hangout of sorts on the wrong side of Times Square. But no hotel on the planet gained as much media attention as the Royalton. Directly opposite the Harvard Club and the Algonquin, the Royalton invented the concept of the hotel as nightclub – a place to hang out, not just to sleep.

Back in the late 1980s the Royalton looked startlingly fresh. The work of Philippe Starck was still novel, as was the idea of dressing the staff in designer clothes. The Royalton was exciting and different and irritatingly irreverent. Guests were treated like shit – and they loved it. It created the impression that this was a place so special it didn't need you.

Now that there is nothing new about design as a hotel ingredient, the peculiarities of the eighties seem exactly that. Design is still a crucial component in any successful contemporary hotel, but the pendulum has swung back, and the name of the game is balance – between what the hotel looks like and what it's like to stay in. That means the quality of the service is just as important as the pedigree of the couch. Sure, staff can wear designer outfits, but it's no longer enough that they are so good looking you don't want to ruffle their cool by asking them to carry your suitcase.

In the completion of one cycle and the beginning of another, there's symbolic justice in the fact that the hotel that defines the new style has opened across the street from the Royalton. The City Club is not the creation of a nightclub impresario or a real estate developer, it's the brainchild of first-time hotelier Jeff Klein, who rightly spotted a gap in the ever-expanding market of hotels that use design to differentiate themselves.

With their ornate ceilings, City Club's duplex suites may be the most memorable guestrooms in Manhattan

A modern version of the eighteenth-century cabinet of curiosities adds character to the tiny lobby

Abstract photography introduces color and atmosphere to the small restaurant space

A large paper mobile by graphic design guru Fabien Baron floats over the double-height lobby

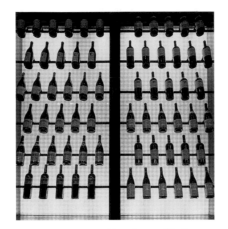

The wine cellar of DB Bistro Moderne, City Club's acclaimed restaurant, is backlit with a funky yellow glow

Nothing about City Club's design is predictable. Artworks are arranged not along the corridors but at the corners

Klein recognized that important as beautiful and interesting rooms are, it's also nice when the hotel restaurant is acclaimed for its food and the staff for their service. When you go downstairs to dine in the City Club's restaurant, DB Bistro Moderne, you'll experience some of the best cuisine available in Manhattan right now. Daniel Boulud is New York's equivalent of a starred Michelin chef, and the nightly scramble for tables is typically New York: frantic and insistent. Of all the dishes, the signature DB burger is the one to have, a generous flying saucer of prime ground beef filled with a center of foie gras. How American, how New York, how decadent. Better still, this sought-after restaurant is the same kitchen that provides room service. The ultimate in up-to-the-minute Manhattan decadence is to borrow one of City Club's vast collection of DVDs, pop it into your sophisticated flatscreen TV, plop back on your Frette linen-covered down pillows and order the DB burger from room service. To round it out, be sure to book one of the duplex suites with a living room on one floor and a bedroom on the next, below an ornate, late-Victorian wedding cake of a ceiling. The two levels are connected by a winding staircase reminiscent of the spiral stairs designed by Le Corbusier for the Comte de Beistegui in Paris. With extraordinary classic windows reaching the full two stories, these have to be the most glamorous hotel rooms in New York.

City Club is not a big hotel, but it is large in ambition. Jeff Klein intended to make this the best individual hotel in New York, and as such he pulled no punches. He hired interior designer Jeffrey Bilhuber, who has also worked for David Bowie and Anna Wintour, and commissioned artworks from some of the biggest creative names in New York. It's true that not all of it works. The Fabien Baron-designed paper mobile that hangs in the double-story lobby, for example, is regularly disarrayed by incoming blasts of wind. But you have to admire the courage of someone willing to think so big, even if on a small scale.

address City Club Hotel, 55 West 44th Street, New York, NY 10036
t +1 (212) 921 5500 **f** +1 (212) 944 5544 **e** info@cityclubhotel.com
room rates from $225

60 thompson

"I'm sorry sir, but that's it. I'm afraid I'm going to have to ask you to leave." It was just before midday on a quiet Sunday in Manhattan and I was busy taking pictures in Thom, the ground-floor restaurant of 60 Thompson, the newest hotel in ultra-hip SoHo. "What do you mean?" I replied, "I haven't finished." "I mean you have been here for well over an hour, guests are starting to arrive for lunch, and I want you out." At first I thought the restaurant manager was joking, but not so. "I haven't finished," I repeated, "you do know this photography is for Hip Hotels, don't you?" "Yes sir, you already told me that, but frankly you are in the way and if you don't leave I'll have security remove you." I was a little put out, I admit, and left Thom not entirely of my own accord.

Why repeat such a sorry saga? Because once I had cooled off it dawned on me that here was good news for the guest – proof that the phenomenon of the designed-to-the-teeth hotel or restaurant has finally turned the corner. In the old days, the media was king. If the photographer from *Vogue* wanted the restaurant empty, it was empty. If there was a fashion shoot to be held in the bar, bye-bye drinkers. There was always a fresh supply of customers – the media exposure ensured it – but the press might

not come back. But that was when there were perhaps three design-conscious hotels in New York City. Now there are more than I can keep track of, with new ones opening every other week. Things have definitely changed. Not only have independent, design-aware hotels become more professional, but the laws of economics have hit home: clients are a finite commodity after all. Suddenly the new criteria are the old criteria. The guest is once again king.

60 Thompson is the latest project by the Pomeranc Group, a company that started out in the 1950s and expanded its real estate ventures to include a fat portfolio of airport hotels. Thompson is its first luxury project, but the experience of building and managing normal hotels is definitely no disadvantage. Ironically, given its ideal location on a rare quiet stretch right in the heart of SoHo, this project was originally meant to be uptown on the West Side, in the exact location of the Hudson Hotel in fact. The people at Pomeranc had set their hearts on this Upper West Side building only to discover, at the eleventh hour, that they had been outbid by Ian Schrager. Feeling thoroughly dejected, Jason Pomeranc and his brothers took a cab downtown to have lunch at SoHo's Lucky Strike, and it was

while they were dining that they noticed a "for sale" sign on a rundown garage across the street. Not only was the location perfect, but it offered the opportunity to knock down and start from scratch – a plus for a real estate developer, because it not only makes a project cheaper and quicker, it offers the chance to custom-design.

At thirteen stories, 60 Thompson is one of the highest buildings in the area, and the planning stage was not without its hurdles. In order to secure permission to build high, New York property law dictated that Pomeranc and his brothers had to buy "air rights" from all their neighbors. "I own all the air on this block," Jason Pomeranc jokingly boasts. At least he is able to laugh about it now. Size aside, 60 Thompson is also no slouch when it comes to design. The architect who designed the building, Steven Jacobs, was a pioneer in turning SoHo and Tribeca's industrial spaces into residential lofts. For the interiors Pomeranc turned to Thomas O'Brien, head

of Aero Studios, whose past work includes apartments for high-profile clients such as Giorgio Armani and Donna Karan. The interiors take their cue from the work of Jean-Michel Frank, but O'Brien's primary inspiration for the lobby space – a long rectangular hall on the second floor (first floor if you are European) – was, oddly, an old photo of Burt Lancaster lounging on an impossibly long couch at his home in Malibu. Hence the deep-buttoned velvet banquette that stretches the entire length of the hotel. The design of the guestrooms isn't quite so original – I've seen similar in Paris – but they are very comfortable and, importantly, quiet. As is increasingly the norm, the high-tech end is well catered to, with a DVD-playing television and broadband internet access. Being one of the tallest buildings in SoHo also means there are great views from the hotel's rooftop, where the terrace bar has become a SoHo summer destination in its own right. As for the restaurant manager – let's just say he's not on *my* Christmas card list.

---

address 60 Thompson Street, New York, NY 10012

t +1 (212) 431 0400 **f** +1 (212) 431 0200 **e** info@thompsonhotels.com

room rates from $259

estrella

Palm Springs, even residents will agree, is both sublime and ridiculous. Some places, like Miami Beach, have become kitsch over time, but Palm Springs was that way right from the beginning. This desert town, framed by the San Jacinto Mountains, has been a magnet for creative and flamboyant individuals since the early 1920s. It first attracted arty types in the early years of the twentieth century; then came the Hollywood invasion in the 1930s. By the 1940s the town had come to symbolize the all-American love of perfect weather and golf, spiced with a reputation for decadence, even seediness. This yin and yang was like catnip for the stars. Palm Springs lured the likes of Bob Hope, Dinah Shore, Lucille Ball, Desi Arnaz and Bing Crosby as well as movie moguls such as Darrell F. Zanuck. Here they built spacious air-conditioned compounds with glamorous swimming pools, and hosted the kind of parties that have lived on in gossip columns ever since. A lot of the antics of the now infamous Rat Pack took place in Palm Springs.

By the 1970s the glamour and glitz had long faded. The town's central thoroughfare, Palm Canyon Drive, had turned into a strip of cheap restaurants and T-shirt shops. The 1980s weren't any better. This was the era of the snowbirds – tourists from snowbound places like Chicago, desperate for some sun and warmth. Since the early 1990s, however, Palm Springs has been experiencing a boom that is starting to resemble the one of the 1940s. A collection of "reputation" restaurants now dominate Palm Canyon Drive, and the visionary architects who originally turned Palm Springs into a modernist playground – Frey, Schindler, Neutra – have been rediscovered and their properties renovated and restored. This desert town is once more a fashionable escape destination for well-heeled Los Angeles society.

With such a resurgence it was only a matter of time until the team of LA property developer Brad Korzen and interior designer Kelly Wearstler opened a hotel here. In early 2003 Estrella joined the ranks of the new-generation Palm Springs hotel destinations. Outside, the design is mid-century motel mixed with California Mission style, exactly the kind of exterior that David Lynch is fond of – a place with the kind of Southern Californian blandness that gives nothing away. So the interior is quite unexpected. Rather than the mid-century modernism of Orbit In, or the multicultural eclecticism of Korakia, Wearstler opted to re-evoke the glamour of Hollywood's golden age.

Estrella's Hollywood Regency style is a theatrical version of old European aristocratic decor: lots of chandeliers, formal drapery, Regency-style dining chairs. The difference is that it is all executed in a manner more sympathetic to the American spray-and-wipe culture. Regency chairs are upholstered in white vinyl, cabinets are painted and given a bit of mirror inlay, and the chandeliers hanging above the table have not a trace of crystal – nothing to clean, nothing to break. Guestrooms are sparkling white spaces accented with an oversize Greek key pattern, the odd splash of black-and-white houndstooth, 1960s reproduction Regency armchairs upholstered in bright yellow, whitewashed urns, plaster medallions and white Flokati rugs. Take a room from a splendid French chateau or townhouse, dip all the contents in white paint (give or take the odd citrus splash), lower the ceiling, shrink the space and you start to get the idea.

In practically any other setting Hollywood Regency would be a dubious design route, but in Palm Springs it works like a gem. Estrella's seventy-four rooms are spread out over a variety of studios, suites and private villas. Wearstler's Hollywood glamour approach has transformed what would otherwise be a collection of architectural non-events into a collage of stylish accommodation options.

Estrella seems to market itself particularly for weddings, which apparently have become a big thing in Palm Springs in recent years. Perhaps it's because of all the white, but there's also a certain theatricality to this hotel that goes beyond the Hollywood Regency interiors. The hotel grounds, for instance, are landscaped in a Beverly Hills movie mogul manner with three swimming pools (two for adults only), lots of palm trees, plenty of potted topiary, and enough ceramic whippets to fill a kennel. In the hands of a designer less confident than Wearstler, all this could so easily be a formula for camp overkill, but she manages to pull it off. Kitsch in the right hands can be a good thing.

---

address Estrella, 415 South Belardo Road, Palm Springs, California 92262

t +1 (760) 320 4117 **f** +1 (760) 323 3303 **e** info@estrella.com

room rates from $159

168

korakia

When I first heard about this hotel I was skeptical. It has had great press over the years, but it looks so Moroccan. Why not build in the style of the region? But admittedly I had never been to Palm Springs, so I just didn't get it. Once I did go there, it didn't take long. There's something about Palm Springs that is strongly reminiscent of Morocco. Perhaps it's the heat, or the palm trees, or the desert that glows red at sunrise and sunset; perhaps it's the laid-back rhythm of a lifestyle where people don't really venture out until the heat of the day has abated.

For lovers of Palm Springs mid-century modernity, Korakia is not for you. But if you are seeking a seductive retreat from day to day reality, it's perfect. The keyword is romance. Unlike the slick air-conditioned atmosphere of most American luxury hotels, this is a place of handwashed linen sheets, canopied four-poster beds, of lace, ceiling fans, slate and wooden floors, furniture from Rajasthan, chairs from Mexico, glassware from France, black-and-white photography and lots of old books. Following a spectacular sunrise (pretty much guaranteed in Palm Springs), the day starts with breakfast in the garden. Small, weathered wooden tables are set with blue gingham cloths and in the shade of citrus trees you are served strong coffee, toast, pastries and homemade blueberry pancakes. Suddenly the Los Angeles of freeways and fast food seems a million miles away. By night, the impression is of being on the set of Bertolucci's *The Sheltering Sky*. Candlelight flickers, the pool glows between palm trees, and the lights from the guestrooms peek out through small, typically Moroccan windows onto a complex of courtyards and outdoor plazas.

It's a romantic place with an equally romantic past. Dar Marroc, as the villa was originally called, was built in 1924 by the Scottish artist Gordon Coutts in memory of his beloved Tangier. This was Palm Springs before it was discovered by the movie crowd. It was still primarily an artists' colony and the domed desert hideaway of Coutts' Moroccan folly, with its whitewashed battlements and huge wooden doors, became its cultural center. Diverse artists came from all over the world to visit Coutts and his young wife Gertrude. The flamboyant artist, with his flaming red hair, would tell tall tales of his exotic travels against the spectacular setting of the San Jacinto Mountains. His bohemian guests included Rudolph Valentino and Errol Flynn. Even Winston Churchill is rumored to have painted in the artist's studio that today is one of Korakia's guestrooms.

Palm Springs' little bohemian secret might eventually have been forgotten had it not been bought fifty years later (albeit in a dreadful state) by another international adventurer, Los Angeles native Douglas Smith. Smith had lived a life every bit as cosmopolitan as Coutts, and what's more he even resembles the younger Coutts. Raised in the suburbs of LA, Smith fled to Newport Beach for a life of racing and skippering yachts along the California coast, before moving to Paris – as Coutts had before him, to study art at the Julian Academy. Smith eventually landed up on the Greek island of Spetses, where he opened the Kalla Café, a big favorite with jetsetters like Jackie O., Mick Jagger and Stavros Niarchos. He returned to the States in 1979 to work as an architect and designer. But just as Coutts had pined for Morocco, so Smith longed for the simple beauty and whitewashed architecture of his Mediterranean hideaway. Palm Springs reminded him of Spetses, and he started to look there for a piece of property for his wife and daughter. That he should end up with Coutts' Tangier-inspired folly was the stuff of a Danielle Steel novel. Needless to say, it took a lot of work to restore the original fiber of the villa. But Smith, with his training in design and his worldly experience, was perfectly placed to provide the property with the type of aesthetic that feels as if it's always been this way: not designed, just right. The Moroccan architecture is still evident, but to that Smith has added the influence of the American Southwest, of Mexico, and of the whitewashed walls of Greece – a mixed bag to be sure, but a successful one because all these influences share a common spirit. The style also now extends to the neighboring property, a 1937 Mediterranean-style villa built for the early screen star J. Carol Naisch, which Smith has restored and made part of Korakia.

Style aside, the real secret of Korakia's success is that it reminds you of wherever your own strongest romantic memories were forged. And what could be more romantic than that?

---

address Korakia Pensione, 257 South Patencio Road, Palm Springs, California 92262

t +1 (760) 864 6411 **f** +1 (760) 864 4147

room rates from $129

orbit in

Bing and Bob did it. So did Frank and Dean. For a couple of decades Palm Springs lured the biggest names in show business to come and live in this barren patch of hot rocky desert two hours east of Los Angeles. Why? Why would household names with enough money to live anywhere settle for this sunscorched outcrop? Because unlikely though it may now seem, for a while this was the brave new world. In the years before and particularly after World War II, Palm Springs was a hotbed of American innovation. War had bred a distaste for the past; modern was the new must, and nowhere was more modern than Palm Springs. Architects Richard Neutra, Rudolf Schindler and Albert Frey, industrial designer Raymond Loewy – all the big names in American architecture and design worked here. Some also chose to live here: Swiss-born Frey built for himself a groundbreaking house that barely touches the earth it stands on, as well as an avant-garde gas station straight out of *The Fountainhead*. For designers this was where the modern dream was being realized, a setting for lightly built open-plan structures largely in glass. With wealthy clients lining up with commissions, and no historical precedents to constrain them, there was freedom in "them thar hills."

The sense of freshness and openness did not last – perhaps always the way with style and design – but it flourished for long enough to make its mark. Palm Springs' current resurrection coincides with the recent reappraisal of what is loosely called mid-century modernism. All of a sudden, chairs, tables and couches that not so long ago you would have had trouble offloading at a garage sale are fetching decent prices in auction houses, and properties by architects such as Neutra and Schindler have re-entered the real estate arena as irreplaceable masterpieces. Film directors and fashion names are scrambling to buy the few remaining unrestored houses that have survived decades of neglect. Tom Ford of Gucci owns one, as does actress Laura Dern: rescuing a Palm Springs mid-century masterpiece has become a very prestigious endeavor. In the process the culture of Palm Springs has changed from one of innovation to one of preservation. But if the money is more conservative, one senses that the investment will be longer lasting.

The story of Orbit In, a collection of typical mid-century apartments around a pool, is classic new Palm Springs. The owners used to be in the natural food business in Portland.

179

Orbit In has one of the best locations
in Palm Springs, nestled at the foot
of the San Jacinto Mountains

Integrity and authenticity are keywords
of the design. Kitchens have original
fittings and 1950s melmac dinnerware

Design details like this atom clock recall
the often overlooked playful side
of postwar modernism

Most of the rooms have a tiny private courtyard complete with a Dean Martin-style cocktail bar

Colorful and comfortable, the guestrooms pack a lot into a small space – they feel more like mini-apartments

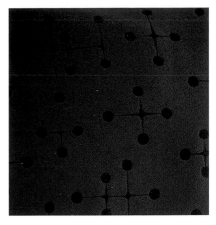

Even the fabrics are faithful to Orbit In's mid-century modern heritage – this is an original design by Ray and Charles Eames

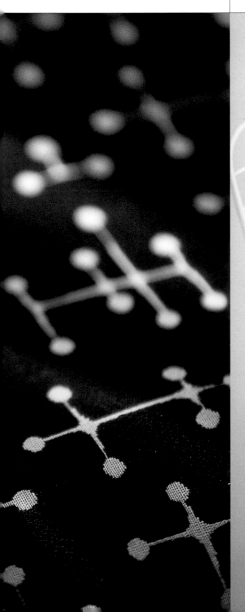

They would come to Palm Springs to escape the rain and gray skies of the Portland winter. On a stroll around one of the most attractive parts of Palm Springs, near the slopes of the San Jacinto Mountains, Christy Eugenis and Stan Amy came across this run-down motel, then called the Village Manor. They hadn't any real desire to own a hotel, but the creative challenge of restoring Herbert W. Burns' property to its former style was a temptation too great to resist.

They bought it "from an eighty-year-old man on oxygen" in July 1999. By that time the only saving grace of the property – which frankly could have won a "most likely scene for bizarre crime act" competition – was the fact that no one had ever spent any money on it. Benign neglect meant that the original fiber of the building was still there for the saving. The man Eugenis brought in for this task was architect Lance O'Donnell. A native of the area who grew up in a modernist house, O'Donnell came to the project with strong convictions. He mourned the widespread destruction of the modernist legacy of a town that arguably has the greatest collection of mid-century houses in the world. To him Orbit In was an opportunity to salvage "a Hollywood starlet with great bones – she may have been a bit wrinkled but she was still beautiful underneath." Thus, outside and in, the place was lovingly returned to its Rat Pack glamour days. Furniture and fabrics from the studio of Ray and Charles Eames, framed 1950s album covers, cocktail bars, atomic-inspired wall clocks, lava lamps, Bertoia chairs, mix and match melmac dinnerware: all was painstakingly assembled in order to create an interior faithful to the building's origins.

But does all this make Orbit In a museum reserved for architecture buffs who come to visit all those widely published houses of Palm Springs past masters? Hardly. The message for guests is clear: it's not just 1950s content that has been recreated here, but 1950s attitudes. This is one motel where you can still smoke, drink, sunbake and party just like Sammy, Frank and Dean.

address Orbit In (the Oasis), 562 West Arenas, Palm Springs, California 92262

t +1 (760) 323 3585 **f** +1 (760) 323 3599 **e** mail@orbitin.com

room rates from $209

the hideaway

When asked which was his favorite project, Frank Lloyd Wright always replied: "the next one." This, I'm convinced, is the true spirit of an artist – what's done is never right, and the motivation to keep working is to improve on what came before.

Christy Eugenis had done extremely well as the designer and proprietor of Orbit In. Not only is her revamped 1957 motel a hit with Palm Springs visitors, but the press love it too. The *Boston Globe* hailed the renovated hotel as "surpassing its former fifties glory;" the *Hartford Courant* proclaimed it "a Mecca for mid-century design, a Lourdes for the revival of Desert Modernism" – a bit on the purple side, but you get the idea. And *Time* magazine called it "meticulously restored and impeccably decorated," and even went as far as to say "it's hard to imagine another hotel whose dedication to design is so intense." Intense is exactly the right word – it captures the extraordinary focus that Eugenis brings to her Palm Springs pursuits. She had previously had a varied career as a real estate agent, a sportswear designer, and a vintage clothing store owner, but her affinity for mid-century modern design has made her one of Palm Springs most successful new hoteliers.

Eugenis and her architect Lance O'Donnell did a great job and got all the accolades they deserved. Most would happily have left it at that. But coming across an article about Burns' first Palm Springs motel in a 1948 issue of *Architectural Record* stirred up a "let's do it again" euphoria. Before you could say Herbert W. Burns, Eugenis had acquired the place. The old Town and Desert Inn came with an even greater design pedigree than the Orbit. It had been extensively photographed in its heyday by Julius Shulman, the recently rediscovered master of mid-century Californian architectural photography. Armed with his original black and white pictures of the exteriors, the pool, the courtyard and the interiors, Eugenis embarked on another renovation, this time with the express aim of exceeding her previous results.

It was a tall order, but she succeeded. The Hideaway is not necessarily better than the Orbit, but it's certainly different. First from an architectural and design point of view, it is purer. In black-and-white photos, it's difficult to tell the 2003 version from the 1948 one, which is exactly what Eugenis was aiming for. She went to remarkable lengths to recreate the original look and style of the place, including

sourcing a collection of Aimes Aire pool furniture. Interior furniture by modern masters Eames, Bertoia, Risom, Paulin and Breuer was mainly collected in Palm Springs by Eugenis herself. Then in a nice twist, she purchased Shulman's original pictures and used them to decorate the interiors.

The seagrass on the floor is the same as at Orbit In, but in terms of detail that's pretty much where the parallels with its sister motel end. The original Orbit In was intended to be fun, sociable and colorful, with a touch of Rat Pack-esque debauchery, but the Hideaway is for purists – connoisseurs who like their modernism authentic and peaceful. Thus while the Orbit has a certain buzz, there's a confident calm at the Hideaway. In keeping with its low-key intent, there's no sign outside, not even a little one. It looks like a perfectly preserved modernist apartment complex, or perhaps a bungalow, but certainly not a hotel. The Hideaway has no lobby, no reception desk, in fact no public spaces at all unless you count

the living room at the other end of the complex, which looks uncannily as it does in Shulman's 1940s photographs.

Of the two Eugenis projects, the original Orbit In is undoubtedly more fun, but even so I prefer the Hideaway. Its atmosphere gives a rare insight into the spirit of refinement and ease that the architecture and design of this period could achieve. Staying in this neutrally toned, perfectly groomed piece of mid-century design you really start to understand what all the fuss was about. This place has real artistic integrity – a fact not lost on the New York-based art photographer I ran into while I was there. She and her model were traveling the area seeking to capture mid-century moments. There could be no more perfect setting for their enterprise. While I was busy photographing the interior, she had her model pulling down his swimsuit by the edge of the pool. On Polaroid it definitely looked like a martini moment – or rather, a post-martini moment. Art imitating life: surely a telling endorsement.

address The Hideaway (Orbit In), 370 West Arenas Road, Palm Springs, California 92262

t +1 (760) 323 3585 **f** +1 (760) 323 3599 **e** mail@orbitin.com

room rates from $189

kennedy school

Leave it to Beaver, My Three Sons, The Brady Bunch – anyone who grew up on a diet of all-American family sitcoms will recognize this setting: suburbia USA. The least likely place for a Hip Hotel. In truth I was pretty wary. Having grown up in American suburbia, I couldn't see the appeal. Driving through the grid of neatly manicured residential streets, each with their quarter- or half-acre plots of front lawn, driveway and garage, my thoughts rested on the improbable prospect of spending the night in an elementary school. But curiosity is a powerful motivator, and I persisted despite some nagging concerns – like the height of the washbasins, for starters.

But if the venue of Kennedy School is suburban, its transformation is a triumph of imagination. Architecturally speaking, it is a handsome brick building with tile and stucco detailing. It's a formal structure that reflects the intention of the local entrepreneur who commissioned it in 1915 as a philanthropic gesture to his community. He wanted to build a worthy school, and it's a testament to his vision that the building has lasted so well. Architectural quality and constructional integrity aside, however, by the late 1990s it was scheduled for destruction. A new school

had been built nearby and Kennedy was redundant. Without much expectation, the City Council nonetheless invited bids for commercial projects that might save the building. At first the suggestion of converting it to a hotel was as puzzling to the Council as it was to me. Somehow drinking, smoking, eating and sleeping – particularly in the Biblical sense – seemed altogether inappropriate in a building whose purpose had been to shelter and educate pre-teen innocents. Not many other offers surfaced, however, and the team from McMenamins – a brewery, restaurant and hotel development group who have also converted a boarding house, a mill and a farm into hotels – were granted their application.

What's most interesting about the resulting hotel is how distinctly it retains the sense of having been a school. Guestroom walls are dominated by the original blackboards, which slide up to reveal the wardrobe storage where once children hung their coats and stored their bags. More tongue-in-cheek, the former detention room is now a smokers' bar with appropriately decadent furnishings for a new generation of American delinquents. The school's auditorium is now a movie theater, but a far more relaxed one than the norm.

Kennedy School's symmetrical architecture is the perfect foil to the eccentric bric-a-brac of the interiors

Old couches and easy chairs furnish the former school auditorium, which is now a hip movie theater

Much to the new proprietors' credit, they preserved the ambience as well as the architecture of the school

In the guestrooms, school blackboards sit alongside white linen, embroidered pillows and Balinese bedheads

Built in the 1920s, this handsome, classically-inspired building was originally an elementary school

The eclectic furnishings of Kennedy School resemble the spoils of a school trip to the fleamarkets of the world

It plays host to a film festival each year, and its furniture is a cozy assemblage of old couches and deep armchairs in which you are absolutely encouraged to slouch. Immediately next door is a bar that bakes pizzas, makes fresh popcorn and serves beer from a keg, all of which you are invited to take into the theater with you. The basketball gym is used for wedding receptions, the former playground hosts an outdoor brasserie and the principal's office is the reception.

But what decorative style is appropriate to a converted elementary school? Anything too chic or sophisticated would destroy the ambience; anything too simple might serve to bring back disagreeable disciplinarian memories. Whether on purpose or by accident, McMenamins certainly hit on the right formula with an eclectic array of furnishings, objects and fabrics from all over the world: Thai statues, Turkish samovars, Spanish tiles, art nouveau flourishes, Indian silks, Mexican silver – almost as if a whole bunch of adults had gone on a grown-up school trip and returned with their haul for show and tell.

The hotel is a success on many levels. Not all locals welcomed the redevelopment plans at the beginning, but they now make enthusiastic use of Kennedy's restaurants, bars and movie theater, not to mention finding it a handy alternative for putting up visiting in-laws. American guests are fascinated to stay in a school probably not too dissimilar from the one they attended, and for overseas visitors the Kennedy School represents a fun and informative insight into American life.

In so many ways, Kennedy remains a typical American elementary school, very like the one I went to myself. (And yes, the urinals in the boys' room are still at knee height.) But the best thing about staying here is undoubtedly the poetic sense of vindication it gives its adult guests. You are back at school, but this time you can do anything you want – drink, smoke, leave your vegetables, kiss the girl next to you, and no one can tell you off.

---

address   Kennedy School, 5736 NE 33rd Avenue, Portland, Oregon 97211

t +1 (503) 249 3983   **f** +1 (503) 288 6559   **e** general@kennedyschool.com

room rates from $99

hotel lucia

What does it take to distinguish a hotel these days? Sometimes a lot, and sometimes very little. But in an age when there is less and less to differentiate one metropolis from another, emphasis on local personality – on making a point of the fact that you are somewhere in particular – is bound to grow.

When you arrive at the Lucia in downtown Portland, there's seemingly little about it that's identifiably Portland. It's a very handsome hotel, don't get me wrong: the ground floor is elegantly appointed, with an interesting mix of contemporary furniture and some captivating art. The lobby is appropriately hip, with fiber optic lighting that changes its colorwash with metronomic regularity and wall paneling fashioned from a single Sapele tree, an exotic African hardwood. Big flowers are arranged in large modern glass vases, the floors are of gleaming polished stone, and in a quiet corner of dark masculine colors and textures, there's a stainless steel fireplace. It's all very attractive and cutting-edge contemporary – but is it Portland? Certainly it's the only hotel like it in the city – and perhaps, I pondered, that is enough. But I underestimated the people behind this hotel. Because there is a Portland connection, and a powerful one at that.

Throughout the ground floor, all along the corridors, and in the guestrooms, there's a collection of fascinating black and white photographs. These pictures were all taken by one photographer, the official White House photographer through seven presidencies. His name is David Hume Kennerly and – guess what – he's a native of Portland. Artistically speaking, Kennerly is no lightweight. Since starting out on the *Oregan Journal*, his pictures have appeared in *Time*, *Life* and *Newsweek*, among other major publications, and he was awarded the Pulitzer prize in 1972 for his work in Vietnam. His hauntingly memorable repertoire includes such images as President Nixon giving a victory sign as he boards the presidential chopper for the last time following the Watergate scandal, and Russian president Brezhnev in the days of the Cold War. Lucia's corridors are lined with Kennerly's photos of presidents, first ladies and world leaders, as well as candid moments with film and television stars – a fascinating mix. There are even prints hanging in the elevator. The hotel's collection of 680 pictures is larger than the recent Kennerly retrospective at Washington's Smithsonian Institution; it is in fact the biggest collection of Kennerly's work on the West Coast.

So the Lucia is not just a hotel, it is also a permanent gallery to one of Portland's most eminent photographers.

Not too long ago, however, there was nothing remotely remarkable or interesting about this address on Southwest Broadway. (All the downtown streets in Portland, by the way, follow New York's naming and numbering system, but with the very confusing addition of prefixes to indicate which side of the river they lie on. The winding river cuts through many of them more than once – try working that out on your first drive into the city.) Portland's old Imperial Hotel first opened in 1908; by the end of the century the only thing it had going for it was its location in the very heart of the city.

And what kind of city is that, you may wonder. Portland's personality is much more difficult to pin down than that of cities like New Orleans, Miami or New York. One journalist characterized it as the city of "B"s – bicycles, bridges, brewery pubs and bookshops. It's true – everywhere you look, people are reading as they lean against lamp posts, wait for a bus, or perch on a stool in an internet café. From the looks of it, Portland's population must be the most literate in the USA. And maybe it's all that reading that has made them nicer people, too. You can stroll around the center all day long without hearing a single horn honk, even though the traffic is every bit as congested as in any other big US city.

Also like other big American cities, Portland has a Chinatown, as well as a suitably sophisticated restaurant scene. Which takes us back to the Lucia, whose ground-floor Typhoon restaurant has already been hailed as one of the top ten Thai restaurants in the country. Its kitchens also provide room service with a Thai flavor. Typhoon's chef and co-proprietor Bo Lohasawat Kline trained in her native Thailand, where she helped to launch Amanpuri. So there you have it: contemporary style, iconic photography, Thai food, all bang in the middle of a genteel metropolis – who would still stay at the Marriott?

address   Hotel Lucia, 400 SW Broadway, Portland, Oregon 97205

t +1 (503) 225 1717   **f** +1 (503) 225 1919   **e** howard@hotellucia.com

room rates from $115

diva

Blink and you'll miss it. Diva doesn't exactly have an imposing presence on San Francisco's Geary Street. The first time I walked by I thought it was a contemporary furniture shop. Even when I knew better, I didn't investigate any further because of all the cities in the United States, San Francisco probably has the greatest diversity of interesting places to stay. For bookish types there's the literary-inspired Rex, complete with library-style breakfast room. For the rock and roll set, there's the Phoenix, where even roadies (not exactly known for their sensitive side) are welcome – with their trucks. For the style-conscious on a budget there's the Commodore, with its monochrome landmark bar the Red Room. Then there's the rather grand Mark Hopkins for traditionalists, and the Clift for devoted fans of Schrager hotels. And even this list is a much abbreviated version of the possibilities on offer.

Three years were to go by before I made it past the same unassuming but unusual facade again. But this time I did investigate. In a city of individual hotels catering to particular target tastes, Diva is the hotel for dedicated fans of contemporary design: clean and modern, without the frills. With its bold cobalt blue carpets and floor-to-ceiling sculpted stainless steel bedheads, metallic Noguchi-style coffee tables and black leather modern couches, it's a hotel that doesn't really care if a lot of people say "I couldn't possibly stay in a place like that." Hotel Diva is different, and that is its strength.

As is often the case, the impression of simplicity belies the sophistication that went into creating this interior. The streetfront facade, for example, may be small but it is strikingly unusual. It is glass, that much is clear (no pun intended). But its refractive quality is due to the fact that it is formed of stacked sheeted glass. Inside, the elegant reception desk is made from a chunk of dark granite with backlit panels of onyx. Proprietor Yvonne Detert, together with designer Olle Lundberg, has achieved an effect that is sleek, sophisticated and space-age, but simple – a white, silver, gray and cobalt-colored statement of originality that more than lives up to the hotel's name.

But aside from its individuality, what else does Diva have to offer? The most obvious answer is location. Shops, theaters, restaurants, bars and nightlife – everything is in walking distance. Turn left out of the hotel entrance and in less than half a block you're on Union

Square, the heart of downtown San Francisco. This is hardly a city where you could be short of things to do, and Union Square is the perfect place to start. You could begin the day by taking a cable car to the top of Nob Hill to see the views over Golden Gate Bridge and Alcatraz. Back in town, one of the best places for lunch is the Grand Café brasserie of the Monaco Hotel, diagonally across the street from Diva. Then in the afternoon you could sample some of San Francisco's abundant Old World gentility, settling in for a proper afternoon tea amid the Rococo splendor of the Westin, one of the city's grandest hotels, which also happens to be right on Union Square. A short walk from the square is San Francisco's famous Chinatown. You can't miss it – the entrance is marked by a huge red gate adorned with Chinese dragons.

For shoppers too, Union Square is the place to be. All the most glamorous department stores are right here – Saks Fifth Avenue, Bergdorf Goodman, Neiman Marcus. The myriad of boutiques for which the city is renowned are on the smaller streets leading off the square. And at night you only have to cross the street to visit some of San Francisco's most popular new restaurants.

That's the beauty of Hotel Diva. It even has a Starbucks right next to reception, and the city's best newsstand just next door to that. Staying here is like having your own slick ultra-modern studio apartment in the very heart of the city – and at a price that usually equates with mediocre out-of-town accommodation.

The San Francisco hotel scene brings to mind a comment by a distinguished architect friend of mine in India, Aman Nath. "These days," he observed, "we are well-off enough to design our lifestyle. It is no longer dictated by need but rather by the desire to imagine ourselves in a particular way. We style our lives." Hotel Diva is for people who like their comfort without fuss and their San Francisco entertainment without in-house obligation.

address Diva, 440 Geary Street, San Francisco, California 94102
t +1 (415) 885 0200 **f** +1 (415) 346 6613 **e** reservations@hoteldiva.com
room rates from $125

the mark hopkins

The Mark Hopkins is an American institution. When James Stewart discovers he suffers from vertigo in the Hitchcock classic of the same name, he tells a friend that means he won't be going to the Top of the Mark for drinks. Watch any American film set in World War II and you are almost guaranteed to hear a reference to the Mark. Departing soldiers came here to raise a final toast, and their wives and girlfriends waved them off from what became known as Weeper's Corner.

In 1939, when George D. Smith decided to convert the top-floor penthouse apartment of his Mark Hopkins Hotel into a cocktail lounge, he wasn't quite convinced that people would travel nineteen floors in an elevator just to have a drink and take in the view. To make sure, he installed a dancefloor and hired a band. Only a few days after the official opening he had to cover the dancefloor up again: they needed the space to accommodate the people who were lining up for hours outside. More than sixty years later, the view is still probably the best in San Francisco – and with the Bay, the Golden Gate Bridge, and the infamous Alcatraz, there's plenty to look at.

My own favorite room, however, is not the Top of the Mark but the Room of the Dons,

a stunning 1920s ballroom with a series of seven-foot-high murals that relate the history of California in high Art Deco style. The name threw me at first: Room of the Dons in Chicago I can understand, but in San Francisco? The penny dropped when I took a closer look: it refers to a Spanish don, a prefix denoting a nobleman or gentleman of military rank. With its pilasters, panels and medallions delicately accented in turquoise, melon and persimmon to complement the murals, and the grand windows dressed in rich drapes of woven damask in teal blue, the room is a powerful expression of the wealth and sophistication that set San Francisco apart from other American cities.

The Mark Hopkins is synonymous with the city and the city's history. Mr. Mark Hopkins was one of San Francisco's famous Big Four railway barons, and this address, Number One Nob Hill, was the location of his forty-room mansion, built – at the insistence of his wife Mary – in a fabulous Gothic style with spires, gables and a profusion of gingerbread ornament. When Robert Louis Stevenson visited San Francisco in 1879 he declared Nob Hill "the hill of palaces, certainly the best part of San Francisco. It is here that millionaires gather together, vying with each other in display."

On her death Mary Hopkins left the house to her second husband Edward T. Searles, an interior designer thirty years her junior, and Searles in his turn bequeathed it to the San Francisco Art Institute to be used as a school and museum. But the great earthquake and fire of 1906 destroyed the Hopkins mansion, leaving only the chimney stacks and the granite retaining wall. The Art Institute built a far more modest structure in its place. Then in 1925, George D. Smith, a mining engineer and real estate investor, purchased the site, knocked down the Art Institute building, and instigated plans to build a luxury hotel. Designed by the San Francisco-based architectural practice Weeks and Day, the nineteen-story hotel was built in a combination of French chateau and Spanish renaissance styles, complete with elaborate terracotta embellishments. It opened in late 1926, and was an immediate hit with San Franciscans and visitors alike.

Since then the Mark has had more than its share of famous visitors. In the 1930s and '40s the Peacock Room hosted top supper club entertainers of the day Betty Grable, Dorothy Lamour, Rudy Vallee and even the exotic Peruvian chanteuse Yma Sumac. In 1961, Soviet premier Nikita Khrushchev stayed in the seventeenth-floor Presidential Suite. For the duration of his visit Russian security guards apparently paced the rooms with clunky Geiger counters – at the height of the Cold War, there was no telling when you were going to be nuked.

Unlike many a grande dame of the hotel world, however, the Mark Hopkins was never allowed to fade. Over the years, the hotel has benefitted from several comprehensive makeovers, the most recent in 2002. All the electronics and telecommunications are right up-to-date, and stylistically the hotel does a great job of balancing the grandeur of a bygone age in the public areas with a more modern, pared-down approach for guestrooms and suites. And one thing has not changed at all: Number One Nob Hill is still the most prestigious address in San Francisco.

---

address Intercontinental Mark Hopkins, One Nob Hill, 999 California Street, San Francisco, California 94108

t +1 (415) 392 3434 **f** +1 (415) 421 3302 **e** sanfrancisco@interconti.com

room rates from $290

inn of the anasazi

I hadn't been to Santa Fe since I was a kid, and to be honest my expectations weren't that high. Driving in from Albuquerque didn't exactly raise them. Take the exit for Santa Fe off the six-lane Interstate 25, as I did, and you will find yourself driving past the ubiquitous parade of retail and fast food franchises that visually pollute the American landscape everywhere you go. Only here they are even worse. Because here, every other building – from Holiday Inn to burger house – is built in the style of a faux Navajo adobe trading post with a huge neon sign outside.

So I was relieved to find that the old center of Santa Fe, the historic Plaza district, is as aesthetically consistent and charming as the outskirts are ugly – just as is often the case with historic European towns. Here the adobe buildings are crafted in a more authentic fashion, and the fact that the Plaza district is a fully pedestrianized zone makes it a very pleasant place to be. Santa Fe is one of the oldest cities in the United States. It had already been the site of Pueblo Indian settlements for centuries when the first Spanish arrived here in the early 1600s. In time, after decades of Indian resistance had been quelled, it became the capital of the Spanish kingdom of New

Mexico. It was taken by the Americans in 1846 during the Mexican–American war, and today is the state capital of New Mexico.

Santa Fe is an impressively situated town, surrounded by breathtaking mountain scenery – but then so too are plenty of other towns in New Mexico, Arizona, Colorado and Utah. What makes Santa Fe unique in the American Southwest is its sophistication. This is the Salzburg of the United States: small, scenic, and culturally confident. In fact Santa Fe has the kind of artistic tradition normally associated with the likes of New York's SoHo or San Francisco's Sausalito. Long before the town became fashionable with today's beau monde – with the likes of Gucci's Tom Ford, the late celebrity photographer Herb Ritts and a host of other film stars and television personalities – Santa Fe was home to the artist Georgia O'Keeffe and legendary photographer Ansel Adams. Both were lured here by the dramatic ancient landscape and the vivid presence of Native American cultures such as the Hopi and Navajo, with their distinctive aesthetic expressed in jewelry, pottery, weaving and architecture. Both artists fought to preserve the character and historic legacy of the town.

Inn of the Anasazi is right in the center of old Santa Fe. This is where all the restaurants, shops, galleries and craft centers are located. There's a museum devoted to Native American art and culture, another to the Spanish colonial legacy, the Georgia O'Keeffe Museum, photogalleries displaying vintage prints of Native Americans, shops specializing in Navajo rugs, boutiques offering buckskin jackets and a small firm of bootmakers that has been in business since the late 1800s. For anyone inspired by the graphic culture of the American Southwest, Santa Fe is shopping paradise.

But aside from its convenience, the real strength of the Anasazi is that it manages to embody all that is good about Santa Fe. The style, predictably, is American Southwest – big rugged floorboards, flagstone paving, ceilings with great rough-hewn beams, a large adobe fireplace in the lobby, and smaller ones in all the guestrooms. Navajo-inspired contemporary murals decorate the hotel's restaurant, and the furniture combines ranch-style proportions with typical Southwest textures such as leather armchairs with a weathered patina and cushions upholstered in traditional woven cloth. Not particularly original, you might say. No, but the interior is saved from cliché by the quality of the execution and by the many touches that reflect a more contemporary Zeitgeist: in the rooms, polished aluminium fruit bowls from cutting-edge design gallery Nambé; in the lobby, a massive steel sculpture enameled in the bright colors of the Native American palette; in the restaurant, equally graphic and colorful plates, minimalist cutlery, and a candle sitting on a bronze twig – even the sugar bowl takes the form of a traditional piece of pottery. From the abstracted carpet design to the polished rounded walls so characteristic of the vernacular architecture of the region, the Inn of the Anasazi is one of those places that manages to get all the details just right, making it the perfect base for exploring and enjoying Santa Fe. Just be sure to avoid the exit that takes you through franchise purgatory.

address Inn of the Anasazi, 113 Washington Avenue, Santa Fe, New Mexico 87501

t +1 (505) 988 3030 **f** +1 (505) 988 3277 **e** reservations@innoftheanasazi.com

room rates from $199

ace hotel

Even for someone who had been living in the wild, this property on Seattle's First Avenue was a bit too wild. For three years, Doug Herrick had been roughing it without electricity or running water in one of Washington State's remote valleys. Then a phone call from two boyhood buddies in Seattle tempted him back to the Northwest's Big Smoke.

Herrick and his friends Wade Weigel and Alex Calderwood had been toying with the idea of opening a hotel in Seattle for some time. They knew exactly what they wanted it to be: a place for people in their crowd, a nest for DJs, writers, directors, architects, designers – people described by *Time* as "fashion conscious urbanites." It had to be an alternative to the run-of-the-mill hotel experience and it had to be affordable. Calderwood and Weigel already had some experience catering to this audience. Calderwood founded the record label Sweet Mother Recordings; Weigel is known in town as the man behind the Cha Cha Lounge; and together they founded Rudy's Barbershop chain. With Herrick's background as a landscape architect in California's Sonoma Valley, it was always going to be a cutting-edge venue.

So when a 1912 brick building on Seattle's First Avenue came up for sale, the three friends,

partners and Seattle natives grabbed the chance to turn late-night "what if?" conversations into reality. The location was perfect, in the middle of Belltown, a stone's throw from the water. This area on the fringes of the city center was the birthplace of grunge. Like New York's SoHo, it was once where the artists lived. No doubt most of them have moved on, but not before giving the neighborhood a street cred that has attracted all the right residents. Belltown is filled with great restaurants like Flying Fish, interesting shops like Mint, design furniture boutiques, and charismatic cafés like Macrina, a combination bakery and coffee house. The building was the right proportion for the trio's budget: not too small and not too big. Since they were not going to change its use, it was also unlikely to pose a planning headache.

Great location, perfect size, it had everything going for it…except the state of the place. As Herrick recalls, "it was a huge, horrible, unimaginably squalid mess." It had been built as a mission for seafaring men – a flophouse for sailors between shipping jobs. But it had degenerated into a boarding house for people who had truly hit rock bottom – junkies, hobos, prostitutes. The building was, to put it politely, severely sanitarily challenged.

Nonetheless the trio bit the bullet. Aside from the state of the building, their other major hurdle was budget. With target room prices of $65 a night, there was never going to be a generous budget for the interior. The in-house joke was "budget? what budget?" Designer Eric Hentz was brought on board to work with the kind of sum normally allocated to one room, not an entire hotel. But he turned that around and made it the strength of the Ace. Imagination is its number one design component. To avoid the impression of clutter, all interior surfaces – the plank floors, the wooden moldings, the rough brick walls – are painted white, and all the typical room stuff – phone, clock radio, remote control, even the television – are also white. The carpet in the corridor is a deep brown coconut husk like a gigantic never-ending welcome mat. Even the lighting – simple cubes of frosted white Plexiglas – could have come from an expensive minimally minded Italian furniture importer. The effect is luxurious, the rates are Walmart.

The end result is so measured, so right, that I would never have known the budget was so tight if one of the owners hadn't told me.

In a country that invented multiple bathrooms, they went quite against the grain and decided that some of the rooms would not even have one. Instead, just down the corridor there are six bathrooms arranged in a neat row, army-style, which the occupants of the fifteen standard rooms have to share. No big deal, actually. The chance of the guests in all fifteen rooms waking up at the same time is next to none, and the bonus is that these six communal bathrooms are much larger and more luxuriously fitted than in any comparably priced roadside motel.

Architectural Record summed up the Ace's design as "embracing both the natural and the machined, the high and the low." In other words, this very cool place is invitingly warm. It's also refreshingly irreverent: instead of the Bible, here you get a copy of the Kamasutra and a packet of condoms.

---

address Ace Hotel, 2423 First Avenue, Seattle, Washington 98121

t +1 (206) 448 4721 **f** +1 (206) 374 0745 **e** reservations@theacehotel.com

room rates from $65

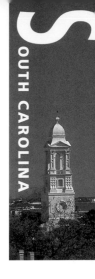
wentworth mansion

The couple who checked in just after me summed it all up: "We're from Chicago," they confessed, "and we know absolutely nothing about Charleston."

To be honest, neither did I. At least I had little idea of Charleston today. For me the town was all about cotton plantations, horse-drawn carriages, classically inspired mansions with lots of shutters and porches – in other words, the Old South of a *Gone With the Wind* cliché. And that's why I was at Wentworth Mansion. Friends had promised me that this huge, classic Victorian pile right in the middle of downtown Charleston was the very embodiment of the Old South.

Once upon a time Charleston was the epitome of Southern prosperity. The city was built by cotton-rich merchants and landowners who used their wealth to indulge a taste for English style and French formality – a seductive blend. But the bloody Civil War put an end to it all. By the time General Robert E. Lee surrendered to those damned Yankees, 600,000 people had died and the South was a smoldering ruin. After telling Scarlett that he doesn't give a damn, Rhett Butler announces that he is going to Charleston "to see if somewhere there isn't something left in life of charm and grace."

He wouldn't have found it. The war had turned Charleston into a charred ghost town, a city of grand widows who without their slaves could never rebuild their former wealth or lifestyle. Once one of the most prosperous places in the New World, Charleston became the forgotten city. While Atlanta established itself as the hub of the modern South, Charleston struggled to find a role. Previously grand townhouses in its old quarter stood empty and dilapidated, casualties of Southern pride – their owners too poor to renovate, but too proud to simply slap on a coat of paint.

When Richard Widman arrived from Los Angeles in the late 1970s he encountered a city without the energy or scarcely even the desire to rescue its crumbling heritage. But Widman saw only opportunity in the tree-lined, slate-paved, mansion-flanked streets of historic Charleston. Against the advice of friends, family and locals, he opened a hotel in a former sailors' hostel in the heart of the threadbare old quarter. Five hotels later it's clear that Widman had glimpsed the Charleston of the future, a city that has come to capitalize on the fact that for almost a century, no one was interested. These days it almost always features in top-ten lists of most desirable city destinations in the US.

Charleston has become one of those American cities, like San Francisco and Santa Fe, that entice visitors by their romance and tradition.

Given that Widman was one of the first to see the tourist potential in Charleston's charm, there's poetic justice in the fact that he has ended up in possession of the city's single most impressive piece of domestic architecture. Wentworth Mansion was perhaps the last grand townhouse funded by cotton money. It was built in 1886 as an opulent private residence for wealthy cotton merchant Francis Silas Rodgers. He spared no expense in either scale or detail – perhaps as a stubborn demonstration of confidence in the postwar South. He commissioned all the stained-glass windows from Louis Comfort Tiffany; all the hardware was custom-made in bronze and brass incorporating the typical basketweave motif of local craft; floors are elaborately laid in parquet or tile; fireplaces are massive slabs of carved marble; and the walls are dignified with neoclassical fluted pillars in polished mahogany.

Today it's almost as if the property had been sealed in a monumental pickle jar for a century and a half. It hasn't: this effect was achieved through enormous, painstaking effort. The entire house was literally taken apart and put back together again. Widman was willing to stop at nothing to realize his dream of reinventing nineteenth-century Southern hospitality. Take the door hardware: the original owner had certainly splurged on hinges, doorknobs, keypads and locking bolts, but twenty-first-century security requirements presented a conundrum – should Widman compromise style for security, or security for style? He refused to do either. Instead he shipped all the hardware north to a specialist locksmith who converted each and every keypad and doorknob to accommodate modern working locks without altering their historic appearance.

To learn about Charleston, that couple from Chicago and I had truly come to the right place.

---

address Wentworth Mansion, 149 Wentworth Street, Charleston, South Carolina 29401

t +1 (843) 853 1886 **f** +1 (843) 720 5290 **e** bseidler@wentworthmansion.com

room rates from $225

cibolo creek ranch

Big hats, big boots, big stakes, big egos, big ranches, big money – the vast state of Texas conjures some vividly romantic images. Even before *Dallas* brought the Southfork brand of Texas lifestyle into hundreds of millions of homes around the globe, we had exotic expectations of this one-time Mexican territory. Think of Texas and we think of its distinctive longhorn cattle, of ranches the size of small countries, of roping, riding, rodeo-loving cowboys, of dust storms, oil derricks, and self-made millionaires chewing tobacco and riding their horses to the doors of their private planes.

In reality, Texas is much more like the world we inhabit, full of shopping malls, freeways, and a seemingly endless suburban sprawl. Even outside the continually expanding urban areas, Texas these days is more a state of "ranchettes" than ranches. These are not the dusty never-ending spreads featured in the movie *Giant* – more like big suburban houses that happen to have huge yards and miles of neat white fencing.

There really aren't too many big ranches left in Texas. So it's lucky that one of the most authentic and impressive takes paying guests. Cibolo Creek is 30,000 acres of perfection, a three-dimensional expression of all our most

romantic Texas fantasies. Its authenticity is only accentuated by the time it takes to get there. A twelve-hour drive from Houston or four hours from the nearest commercial airport at El Paso, El Cibolo is situated in El Despoblado (literally, the uninhabited), an enormous, virtually empty tract of land in Texas's Big Bend. This is and always was the perfect place to be a cattle baron.

Almost two hundred years ago Milton Faver, or Don Melitón as he came to be known, arrived at the border town of Presidio del Norte, apparently on the run after killing a man in a duel. He married a Mexican woman from an influential family and made some money trading Mexican goods with newly arrived settlers just across the Rio Grande. When the United States army built Fort Davis in Big Bend, it was clear they would need beef and other provisions, and Don Melitón saw his opportunity to launch a cattle ranching venture. The terrain he selected was half-way between the fort and the Mexican border in a mountainous region that benefitted not just from a cooler climate but also from a creek that continued to flow even in the most arid weather. Don Melitón was a meticulous man and he approached the development of his 30,000 acres with more care and forethought than one might expect in the

Wild West. First and foremost, to protect against marauding bands of Apache and the even more ruthless Comanche, he built a rectangular adobe fort with walls over three feet thick. This structure was large enough to house his family and shelter his horses and livestock in the event of a raid. As his operation grew Faver built two more forts (La Cienega and La Morita) and diversified into goats and sheep as well as the famous longhorn. By his death, Don Melitón had indeed become a proper cattle baron.

When Houstonian John Poindexter came across El Cibolo in 1990, it was a pale shadow of its former self. But the creek still flowed, and it was this constant supply of clear fresh water that clinched his decision to pick up where Faver had left off. What was left of the old main fort had been whitewashed, and Poindexter found it surrounded by randomly scattered rusting junk, its fences long since fallen down and its roads barely passable. But Poindexter had made his fortune picking up down-and-out companies and turning them around, so he was

not fazed by the scale of his task. He brought in an army of workers from Mexico to painstakingly reconstruct the three forts using handmade sunbaked adobe bricks. He invested in irrigation, built extensive stretches of dry wall, and reintroduced the longhorn herd.

But Poindexter was interested in recreating the lifestyle as well as the look. So at night all of El Cibolo's guests eat together at one enormous table. Instead of television and telephones (guestrooms have neither) there's coffee around an outdoor open fire after dinner. Rooms have adobe fireplaces and big old frontier beds, verandas are adorned with saddles and colorful horse blankets and the floors are laid with traditional baked tiles.

El Cibolo has the vast untouched landscape, the endless sky, the crystal clear air, and the deafening silence we all crave. This is a ranch where you can rope a calf, climb a canyon, or raft down the nearby Rio Grande. Or you can do nothing at all. Either way, you won't ever get closer than this to your own private Ponderosa.

address Cibolo Creek Ranch, PO Box 44, Shafter, Texas 79850

t +1 (915) 229 3737 **f** +1 (915) 229 3653 **e** reservations@cibolocreekranch.com

room rates from $375, including meals and activities

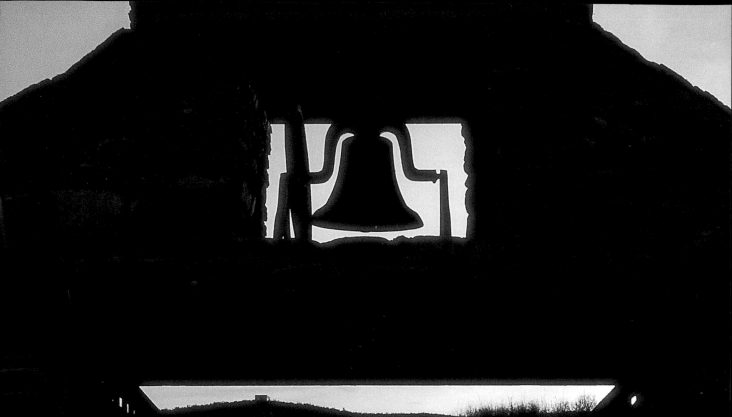

cedar creek treehouse

It's not often you get a national forest to yourself. A few hours southeast of Seattle is the Mount Rainier National Park, a spectacular landscape of dense forest and craggy mountains, and in the middle of it all the imposing snow-capped 14,400-foot peak of Mount Rainier. This is the wilderness that the American Northwest is renowned for, and after the hip urban scene of Seattle, it's a radical and inspiring change.

The spectacle of the park attracts visitors from all over the United States, and so it was when Tennessee-born Bill Compher first came here over thirty years ago. Compher – a cross between Harrison Ford in *Mosquito Coast* and Mel Gibson in *Conspiracy Theory* – loved these forests so much that he stayed. And eventually he realized his dream of building the perfect venue from which to experience them.

Suspended fifty feet up a monster-sized trunk, Cedar Creek Treehouse is in the midst of Mount Rainier's forests. With a babbling brook below and an amazing view from above, you feel like you are hovering above the trees in a silent helicopter, except this is a chopper you sleep in. From up there, as the treehouse sways with the evening breeze, the glaciers of Mount Rainier seem close enough to reach out and touch.

It's an extraordinary retreat – if you can find it. Bill Compher is very determined to keep his best-kept-secret a secret, so he will only send you a map when you confirm your reservation. In my case there was no time for that, so instead he proposed to meet me at the gas station in Ashford, the nearest town. "But," I protested, "I have no idea how long it will take me to get there." The road to Ashford took me right to the other side of the huge national park – an impressive drive to be sure, but not one I would like to put a stopwatch to. But Mr. Compher was insistent, and the gas station in town remained our rendezvous.

Inevitably the drive took longer than it looked on a map. By the time I found the gas station, I was very late – it was beginning to get dark – and I was so tired that a plain old Holiday Inn had started to look quite inviting. So I decided to do my host the courtesy of a call from a pay phone, in view of having missed our meeting, and then find myself a bed for the night. Just as I was pushing the coin into the slot, a bearded mountain man approached and enquired, as if it was the most normal thing in the world, "Excuse me, are you Mr. Ypma?"

It was all too strange. Here I was in the middle of nowhere and Jeremiah Johnson

had just cornered me at the only payphone in town. I started to feel as if I was in one of those "disappeared without a trace" movies. But we shook hands, and without further discussion my host invited me to follow his Polo deep into the surrounding forest. When the paved road ran out and we continued along a dark muddy trail flanked by the occasional empty caravan, I started to hear the banjo music from *Deliverance*.

Eventually we arrived at a clearing in the forest where the rugged path stopped. Peering up, I couldn't see a trace of a treehouse, or any other building for that matter. When my host signalled to me to leave my car in this clearing and proceed on foot, I really started to worry. It was all to do with ecology, he reassured me. He didn't want cars coming too close to his compound, so he had made this the parking lot and built only a slender suspension bridge over the intervening swamp. It was impressive theater, if a little daunting in the pitch-black rustling dark.

Beyond the bridge was another clearing, beside a crystal-clear stream, and the treehouse itself – surprisingly large and unexpectedly high. It will never win design awards for its interiors, but it's all there – a couple of double futons on the upper level, separated by a giant trunk rising through the middle, and on the floor below, a kitchen, a living area, and a sun room from which to enjoy the view. This is not a place where the fluffiness of the towels or the thread count of the sheets is a major factor, that goes without saying. But the constant soothing sway guarantees you will sleep like a baby.

As for my host, the mountain man recluse turned out not only to be a charming and interesting dinner companion, he also had a deft way with understatement. The next morning, he escorted me up a higher tree with rappelling gear and ropes to get a bird's-eye view. As my black Prada shirt and pants got steadily plastered in tree sap, he did quietly remark that I could have been more appropriately dressed.

---

address Cedar Creek Treehouse, PO Box 204, Ashford, Washington 98304

t +1 (360) 569 2991 **e** treehouse@mashell.com

room rates from $250

hotel george

Washington, DC, is probably not a place you associate with groovy lodging. This city, like its international counterparts, Canberra, Islamabad and Brasilia, was built for the job of managing the country. Beautiful as they may be, architecturally significant even, they remain cities of bureaucrats, not likely to stimulate an interesting hotel culture.

Yet a century and a half ago, Washington had what was probably the most exotic hotel culture in the United States. The relatively new republic was in a major growth phase, and to accommodate the throngs of new immigrants, the country was continually pushing to expand its borders. Settlers were enticed westwards with generous land concessions, and frontier territories were being settled and farmed as fast as the DC bureaucracy could make the land available. Only one thing stood in the way of this seemingly unstoppable expansion: the Native Americans. Ancient tribes like the Sioux, the Apache, and the Comanche were none too happy about these free-for-all grabs of what had been their lands, and war would break out whenever the native inhabitants were pushed too far. The solution to the "Indian problem," as it was known, was to entice the

tribes to resettle on new lands which, it was promised, would not be coveted or claimed by the white man. In the long term the US government turned its back on all its guarantees, but in those optimistic early days there was a lot of horse-trading going on in DC. It was in the government's interest to appease the delegations of Indian chiefs who came to Washington to negotiate for their nations in person, and as a result many of the capital's most luxurious hotels regularly hosted tribal chiefs dressed to the teeth in their most impressively elaborate outfits. Wrapped in full bearskins over fringed buckskin trousers with matching shirts, adorned with turquoise and bone bracelets, chokers, and full feather headdresses, toting colorful tribal blankets, these Indian chiefs must have been a magnificent sight.

Of course all that lobbying didn't in the end help the fate of the Native Americans. Slowly, sadly, they disappeared from Washington, DC, just as completely as they had disappeared from their own lands. As for Washington hotels – these days, the odd movie star is as exotic as the clientele ever gets. Washington is a town of conservative and expensive hotels – not an obvious context in which to launch a funky alternative. But that was exactly what Hotel George was always intended to be: a refreshing change from those fusty, long-established traditional hotels. As such, it has worked perfectly. John Malkovich and Alanis Morissette have stayed here, as did the late John F. Kennedy, Jr., publisher of *George* magazine (no relation).

But it would be simplistic to suggest that the George has become a DC hit simply by being different. It's the manner in which it is different that is important. The lobby, for instance, is furnished with Rietveld-designed furniture manufactured under license by Cassina in Italy. Similarly the lamps in reception are classic Arne Jacobsen designs. Clearly, someone has taken a lot of care with the hotel's public spaces, and that is usually a good sign. You certainly know you're in DC when you enter the lobby, where visitors are greeted by Steve Kaufman's acid green painting of the nation's first president. And just in case you didn't get the connection, the painting is

also reproduced in Hotel George's 139 light-filled, uncluttered guestrooms.

True to the style of DC's lobbying culture, the George also features a cigar-friendly billiard room/bar where the politically motivated can work their spin over "stogies" and a sniffer of Armagnac. Even the power lunch has been given an update by the opening of the hotel's next-door restaurant Bistro Bis, a fresh new look at traditional French cooking by acclaimed DC chef Jeffrey Buben. And when all the drinking, smoking and eating have taken their toll, you can make use of the George's comprehensive health center to get you sufficiently detoxed to contemplate doing it all over again.

Situated in a handsome 1928 building on Capitol Hill, the George is a short stroll from all of DC's major attractions. But I suspect many guests are more than happy to leave the hotel as little as possible. It's one positive lesson to be learned from those Native American DC hotel guests: enjoy it while it lasts.

address Hotel George, 15 E Street NW, Washington DC 20001

t +1 (202) 347 4200 **f** +1 (202) 347 4213 **e** rooms@hotelgeorge.com

room rates from $285

canoe bay

Wisconsin? Why go to Wisconsin?

One very good reason is that Frank Lloyd Wright designed no less than two hundred houses here. This was also where he built Taliesin, the groundbreaking compound he used as retreat, design laboratory, showcase, intellectual hub and the counterpart to his winter compound in Arizona, Taliesin West. Wisconsin was the creative breeding ground for Wright's innovative Prairie Style, and yet sadly today the state is better known for its cheese and its football team, the Green Bay Packers. Fortunately, there are enthusiasts keeping the legacy of this great American architect alive. Dan Dobrowolski, proprietor of Canoe Bay, is a self-confessed Frank Lloyd Wright fanatic, and should you have any time to spare after you leave his compound he can provide you with a detailed tour itinerary of all the most important Wright buildings that can still be visited in the state.

Situated in the northwest corner of Wisconsin, a six-hour drive north of Chicago and not too far from Lake Superior, Canoe Bay is located on three private lakes in a setting that is eerily reminiscent of *On Golden Pond*. It's an idyllic situation of virgin forests and pure waters. In fact the privacy and beauty are such that really any old shack would do here. But not for Dan Dobrowolski and his wife Lisa. His laid-back, easy-going style belies a total commitment to aesthetic standards and a mentality more like that of an artist than a hotelier. It was quite a gutsy move, for instance, to design a hotel in which none of the rooms have a telephone, especially given that each guest cabin is quite remote from the next (not to mention the reception house). But Dobrowolski wants his guests to leave behind their city lifestyles. So if you want something from reception, you have to walk there.

The real testament to Dobrowolski's remarkable sensibility is the architecture. One of the most beautiful of Canoe Bay's cabins looks convincingly like a Frank Lloyd Wright design in miniature, and not by coincidence. It was designed by John Rattenbury, one of Wright's best and most trusted students, who still lives at Taliesin West in Arizona. Apart from his own work as an architect, Rattenbury is a senior fellow of the Frank Lloyd Wright School of Architecture. This cabin is essentially a studio in layout, and the design is thoroughly bewitching in its use of materials and intersecting planes

and angles. Indeed, architecturally speaking, it is to a shack what Fabergé is to an egg.

You certainly don't have to be an architecture junkie to appreciate Canoe Bay. Nature is the premier drawing card here. There are kayaks and rowboats in which to explore Lake Wahdoon, and in winter you can ice-skate or go cross-country skiing. The restaurant is almost as spectacular as the scenery, built and furnished in a style that again borrows from Wright (although not in this case designed by Rattenbury). It specializes in stylized versions of local produce: dishes such as shiitake and cremini mushroom soup, locally caught rainbow trout in cranberry butter, and rack of lamb with hazelnut crust.

So just how did Rusk County, Wisconsin, end up with the only Relais & Châteaux property in the American Midwest? Canoe Bay's estate, comprising 280 acres of lush forest and three private lakes, originally belonged to Ezra Cornell, who donated it in 1874 to Cornell University in New York.

Proceeds from the sale of the land and its timber provided funds to construct the university's first buildings. In the 1960s the property was developed as a retreat, but it had fallen into disuse by the late 1980s. Dobrowolski had explored these forests and fished on Lake Wahdoon in his childhood. In 1992 he bought the entire property and left behind his career as an Emmy-award winning meteorologist with ABC and Fox to concentrate on building his vision of a wilderness retreat for grown-ups.

The couples-only policy makes this one of the United States' most romantic retreats. Just how good is Canoe Bay? Well, *Condé Nast Traveler* voted it one of the best three lakeshore hotels in North America, *Travel & Leisure* named it inn of the month, and *Bon Appétit* praised its extraordinary comfort and cuisine. But ask Dan Dobrowolski about his creation and he'll give you a cheeky smile. "What do I know?" he'll reply. "I'm just a guy who lives in the woods."

address Canoe Bay, PO Box 28, Chetek, Wisconsin 54728

t +1 (715) 924 4594 **f** +1 (715) 924 2078 **e** mail@canoebay.com

room rates from $300

HIP™
HOTELS

© 2003 Herbert Ypma

First published in paperback in the United States
of America in 2003 by Thames & Hudson Inc.,
500 Fifth Avenue, New York, New York 10110

thamesandhudsonusa.com

Library of Congress Catalog Card Number
2002111488
ISBN 0-500-28404-0

Printed and bound in Singapore by CS Graphics

Acknowledgments
Photography by Herbert Ypma, with the exception
of pages 28 and 31 (XV Beacon), by Richard
Mandelkorn of Mandelkorn Photography; and
page 58 (the Townhouse), courtesy of the hotel.

Designed by Maggi Smith